Moving To Las Vegas

Moving to

Las Vegas

Theresa A. Mataga
and John L. Smith

Barricade Books Inc.

Published by Barricade Books Inc.
150 Fifth Avenue
Suite 700
New York, NY 10011

Printed in the United States of America.

Book design and page layout by CompuDesign.

Library of Congress Cataloging-in-Publication Data

Mataga, Theresa A.
    Moving to Las Vegas / by Theresa A. Mataga
        and John L. Smith.
            p. cm.
    Includes index.
    ISBN 1-56980-152-5
    1. Las Vegas (Nev.)—Description and travel.
    2. Moving, Household—Nevada—Las Vegas.
    I. Smith, John L., 1960–   .
    II. Title.
    F849.L35.M37   1997
    979.3' 135—dc21

                                                            96-47868
                                                               CIP

        10   9   8   7   6   5   4   3   2   1

For Vincent J. Baginski, Sr.,
my constant companion.

—Theresa A. Mataga

For Emma and Amelia Smith,
who bridge the generations.

—John L. Smith

Contents

Prologue

Living in a Boomtown

When you move to Las Vegas, you can expect certain questions from outsiders.

A popular one is, "Do people actually live there?"

Sooner or later, you will be forced to explain that, yes, you do live there and, no, you don't get your mail at a Strip hotel.

"Is there a blackjack system that works?" is another favorite.

The answer is yes, but only if you own a casino.

In recent years, by far the most often asked question goes something like, "Las Vegas is booming now, but how long can it last?"

It's a fair question, one that my family has been asking about Nevada and Las Vegas since 1881. My ancestors were among those early arrivals who believed it wouldn't last, or at least I must presume that's so, for we never bothered to buy land. I sometimes imagine my great-great-grandparents standing at the dusty roadside of progress with arms crossed and scowls firmly fixed, thinking, "Damn fools. Don't they know this will never last?"

And they were often right, at least as it concerned the gold- and silver-mining districts of Tonopah and Goldfield in central Nevada. If history is any indicator, Las Vegas differs from those played-out mother lodes in one important regard: Its gold mines never close, and—here's the best part—the miners actually dump their own hard-earned ore into the claims.

That's the wonder of an economy based on casinos and tourism, and that's why answering the question is tougher than it seems.

Clark County has doubled and sometimes tripled in population each decade since its incorporation in 1905. Accompanying that tremendous growth and prosperity are some very real problems that residents must deal with each day. From traffic and crime rates to the city's destructive life-style traditions, Las Vegas isn't simply some green-felt utopia on the Mojave desert. Yet it endures and prospers as never before. If its soul is troubled, it also is a place for second chances.

Las Vegas is the fastest-growing community in America. In a slow month, approximately four thousand people arrive with their dreams and goals and big ideas. For some, Las Vegas represents a chance at economic redemption after a lost job in home-towns across the nation. For others, it's a dream factory where on a given weekend they, too, might strike it rich. It's a foolish but seductive dream. Still others are making Las Vegas their retirement home and are taking advantage of the climate and the state's friendly tax structure.

I hope this book answers a few questions about this most amazing city.

—John L. Smith

Introduction

City in Motion

On October 15, 1995, at the ripe old age of sixty-eight, I decided to put excitement into my life, and I moved to Las Vegas. Life in the middle of the desert has been a unique learning experience. Las Vegas residents are enthusiastically awaiting the completion of more than a dozen new resorts and the expansion of many old favorites. The townspeople brace for the impending boom that will bring job growth and opportunities for advancement. Las Vegas is like a butterfly emerging from a cocoon. By the twenty-first century, Las Vegas will spread its wings in bright and colorful glory.

Las Vegas is a city in perpetual motion. It is a melting pot of languages, cultures, and religions, yet everyone shares a common bond. Residents depend on tourists to keep the economy strong; tourists depend on the residents to provide them with a memorable vacation. Both are in harmony.

The Las Vegas that visitors view from their hotel rooms is not the same place southern Nevada residents see, and that is as it should be. Tourists can take a walk on the Strip or visit the downtown area known as Glitter Gulch without taking the time to think about the hard work and planning it took to provide them with a memorable vacation. All they know is, everything will be ready for them when they arrive in Las Vegas.

When visitors touch down at McCarran International Airport, they immediately notice the large, efficient terminal. Their luggage arrives in short order, and limousines and taxis stand by ready to zip them to their hotels. From the front-desk clerks who speed their check-in and the bellhops who carry their bags, to the maids who freshen their rooms and the waiters who take their orders, casino resorts are all about people. The real people of Las Vegas.

Casinos are filled with emotion. People win money, people lose money, people drink too much. It takes a special type of employee to stay cool in such an environment. And there are thousands in the new Las Vegas.

Las Vegas is a land of opportunity for workers and, increasingly, a home-away-from-home for many senior citizens. Seniors like to play video-poker machines, but they also volunteer their time at local hospitals and homeless shelters. You won't find senior ladies sitting at home in their rocking chairs knitting. Southern Nevada is a place for active seniors.

Las Vegas is not without its problems. Traffic congestion is perhaps the biggest malady in the valley, but Strip hotel executives and Regional Transportation Commission officials are planning a $1 billion monorail system that will carry tourists from the airport to the Strip and downtown. Although county planners and state officials have fallen years behind the city's booming population, they continue to work to improve conditions.

The growing crime rate is a concern, the Clark County School District is overcrowded, and the omnipresence of slot machines and neighborhood casinos complicates the southern Nevada lifestyle, but Las Vegas remains a city of hope for thousands of Americans.

From the executive in his million-dollar mansion to the trashman in his humble abode, everyone has a role in making Las Vegas happen. They are the residents of Las Vegas, and they are indispensable. There are times one must wonder what brought the pioneers to the Las Vegas valley more than a century ago and what brings today's travelers to the middle of the desert. The answer can be found in the hearts of the people who live here. They are some of the nicest people you will ever meet.

Do I like living in Las Vegas?

You bet I do.

Would I ever leave Las Vegas?

Don't bet on it.

When I die, scatter my ashes on the desert so they can blow across the valley with the desert wind.

—*Theresa A. Mataga*

1

The Golden Promise

Now that you have decided to live in Las Vegas, you should know something about its history. That's not as easy as it seems, for in Las Vegas, facts blend with legend the way a blackjack dealer shuffles a deck.

Hollywood lore would have you believe that the town was born when New York gangster Benjamin Siegel arrived in the early 1940s, but he was more than a century late in discovering this superheated spot in the Mojave Desert that has long held the promise of riches.

As a mark on a map, this place was first encountered by Spanish explorers in 1829. Before then, of course, there were the Paiute and Anasazi Indians.

Moving toward the coast in search of gold and trade routes, the Spaniards encountered a marshy desert oasis dotted with streams and artesian springs. They named it Las Vegas or "the Meadows."

By 1843, U.S. Army officer John C. Fremont led a caravan through the region. For a time, poorly re-searched histories of the area falsely credited Fremont with discovering Las Vegas.

Next in line were Mormon missionaries, who arrived in 1855 and toiled with the devotion of true believers to carve out a civilization in the desert. They planted gardens and built walls and lasted two years before the climate, living conditions, and unfriendly Paiutes drove them back to Salt Lake City.

With an abundance of water and the region's first mail route, by Nevada's 1864 statehood, Las Vegas station was a stopping-off point for travelers making the long journey from Denver or Salt Lake City out to California.

It was water that attracted Montana Senator William Clark to the southern tip of Nevada when he and a group of investors determined to build the San Pedro, Los Angeles, and Salt Lake Railroad. By the time the tracks crossed the long valley in 1902, the area was inhabited by hearty ranchers, foraging Indians, and poisonous snakes. Las Vegas never was an easy place to live.

Traveling card sharks used rest stops at Las Vegas to take advantage of suckers and simpletons, and the first tent gambling parlors were born. By the time Las Vegas officially took its name in 1905, it already had its share of gamblers and easy women.

Four years later, growing out from the railroad tracks, Las Vegas sported six hotels, a single hardware store, and eleven saloons and brothels at Block 16, the founding fathers' testament to the power and profit of vice. Clark's railroad may have put Las Vegas on the map, but Block 16's Arizona Club and Black Cat Club would define its image for decades to come. Although the townsfolk frowned on dice-dealing and carousing, most benefited by the dollars such activities generated.

Another marvelous myth about Las Vegas is that gambling always has been legal here. Far from it. It was, in fact, illegal but tolerated for much of the early twentieth century. Legalization came in 1931. Not only would the tax revenue generated feed the state's depleted coffers in the early years of the Great Depression, but touting legal casino games was sure to attract the hundreds of workers building Hoover Dam. With gambling illegal in Boulder City near the dam site, the construction stiffs made frequent trips to Las Vegas and Searchlight, where cold beer, hot cards, and willing women were available for a price.

More than 100 years had passed since Fremont drew his map, and there was still no sign of Bugsy Siegel. A decade after legalization, the city had become well known to racketeers hungry to stretch their legs without fear of law enforcement intervention. The El Rancho Vegas was built south of downtown along U.S. Highway 91, and the Hotel Last Frontier with its entertaining jingle, "the Early West in Modern Splendor," appeared a year later.

By then, Siegel had been spotted in Las Vegas. A

founding member of New York's Bug and Meyer mob, Siegel was sent west by his partner, Meyer Lansky, to avoid a murder rap and cinch up the syndicate's horse-wire interests. It was a mission Siegel welcomed, for he fancied himself as movie star potential (he even had a screen test), courted starlets, and loved to pal around with childhood-friend-turned-screen-gangster, George Raft. His fantasy aside, Siegel was an egotistical hood prone to fits of extreme violence.

He also wasn't shy about making offers other men couldn't refuse. When *Hollywood Reporter* founder and original Flamingo developer Billy Wilkerson ran short of cash, Siegel was there to infuse thousands into the project. Siegel, Lansky, and other East Coast mob bosses already owned pieces of the Golden Nugget and El Cortez downtown, and the Flamingo held the promise of a syndicate desert palace. In a matter of months, Siegel's investment ballooned to more than $1 million, but he had even bigger plans for the resort.

It would have riding stables, tennis courts, mature shrubs, and trees. It would feature a swimming pool, opulent rooms, and a fourth-floor suite devoted entirely to himself. And the costs kept climbing.

Siegel's $1 million investment of the mob's money in the Flamingo was a fiasco of the first order. Between theft on the job site and the high prices of construction materials in the months following the end of World War II, he had set himself up as a patsy as costs climbed toward $6 million. To make matters worse, inclement weather and lucky gamblers made the Flamingo's December 1946 opening a financial flop. The casino closed for a short time, then reopened in the spring of 1947 and immediately began making money.

But it was too late for Siegel. His friends had decided that his lack of business acumen would cost him his life. On June 20, 1947, Siegel was murdered at the Beverly Hills home of his gun-moll girlfriend, Virginia Hill.

Siegel's name burned in the psyche of the mob-loving American public. Whenever Las Vegas was mentioned, the infamous Bugsy was sure to be nearby.

Other men have had a far greater impact on Las Vegas than Siegel, but few compare to the quiet craftsmanship of quintessential racketeer-turned-businessman Morris "Moe" Dalitz. Born in Boston in 1899, Dalitz ran rackets in Detroit, Cleveland, and Newport, Kentucky, before joining the western migration of illegal gamblers to the land of the legitimate dice game. Using their friend Wilbur Clark as a front, Dalitz and his Cleveland partners built the Desert Inn in 1950. Using his contacts with Jimmy Hoffa's Teamsters Central States Pension Fund, Dalitz arranged for the purchase and construction of numerous other hotels. To his great credit, he diversified his business interests to include the construction of the first for-profit hospital in southern Nevada, the first large shopping mall, the first successful private golf course, and some of the most successful housing developments in the city's history. Dalitz, who had thrived in a violent racket, died of natural causes at age eighty-nine.

The history of Las Vegas is the story of the influence of many men and one woman, Lady Luck.

There was nutty billionaire Howard Hughes, who arrived by train at night on Thanksgiving 1966. Hughes purchased seven casinos and vast tracts of real estate and was credited, falsely, with ridding the city of the mob by infusing his so-called clean capital. Although much of the media bought the ruse, Hughes was at best an eccentric landlord who in reality built not a single hotel or casino on the Strip.

Of greater importance is Kirk Kerkorian, the Los Angeles native who grew a multibillion-dollar empire from the sales of airplane and aircraft parts in the years after World War II. On his way to becoming a Las Vegas legend, Kerkorian built the world's largest hotel three times (the International in 1969, the MGM Grand in 1973, and the MGM Grand Hotel and Theme Park in 1994).

Other influences include the wildly imaginative Jay Sarno, who dreamed up the themes for Caesars Palace and Circus Circus and had his sights set on building a behemoth 6,000-room megaresort years before anyone dared to dream that big. Today, the 5,005-room MGM Grand makes Sarno look like a visionary.

If Las Vegas has an undisputed king in the 1990s, his name is Steve Wynn. As chairman of Mirage Resorts, Wynn is responsible for employing nearly 20,000 workers. His creativity has shone through with a man-made volcano at the Mirage and a life-size pirate battle at Treasure Island. Wynn also exercises considerable political will at the local, state, and national levels and has become the living symbol of legalized gaming in corporate America.

In 1998, Mirage Resorts opened the posh Bellagio on the former site of the Dunes Hotel. With its multimillion-dollar works of art, Wynn believes Bellagio will signal continued prosperity for Las Vegas and will remake the city as a playground for the world's well-heeled traveler.

What is more certain is the fact that Las Vegas will continue to prosper economically as long as the gambling industry continues to expand. That economic prosperity, however, has not translated into smart planning on the part of the community's power-brokers and politicians.

The need for smart planning and fast action have never been more urgent. Prior to World War II, a local political structure barely existed.

The first attempt at Las Vegas-style comprehensive planning occurred in 1953 when county officials created a land use guide. The city followed suit in 1959 with the General Master Plan. Everything from annexation and land use to the water supply and sewer system was addressed. And promptly forgotten. Southern Nevada's developers and casino men were too busy growing and making money to worry too much about planning.

Nearly 40 years would pass before the county's so-called Smart Growth Program would signal an era in which planned growth was beginning to be taken seriously. By then, the image of Las Vegas as a growth center had started to suffer under the weight of fears of too little water, a rapidly decreasing quality of air and a diminished quality of life for residents. Casino men and even some developers jumped on the slow-growth bandwagon.

The Las Vegas Valley Water District is in the process of constructing a second pipeline from Lake Mead in order to better serve customers. Key state Legislators such as Sen. Dina Titus have played a big role in forcing the growth agenda not only at the state but also at the local levels. Titus and others have advocated setting specific growth boundaries within the Las Vegas Valley similar to the plan in use in Portland, Oregon. The Ring Around the Valley idea continues to be controversial in growth-crazed Las Vegas, but Titus has vowed to continue to fight to curtail unchecked development.

Growth and development on the Strip became such a hot issue in early 1999 that MGM President J. Terrence Lanni, one of the most respected men in the casino business, publicly suggested a moratorium on new hotel rooms unless planned megaresorts removed older rooms from the city's burgeoning balance. With 126,000 hotel rooms expected to be available before the turn of the century, Lanni's concern appeared justified. "There's going to be a capacity problem, there's no doubt about that," Lanni said.

As with all things in Las Vegas, the bottom line is what the top members of the powerful casino industry think. It was ever thus, and ever thus will be.

Whether you believe the old gamblers got out or simply grew up doesn't matter, really. Today, Las Vegas is as legitimately corporate as any place in

America. And it prospers as never before, thanks to the continued explosion of growth in the casino districts and throughout the valley.

Las Vegas exists almost as much in the eye of the American psyche as on any map. As a city, it defines the present. It is electric and illusory, shallow and symbolic. With its notorious past, its city fathers bury its history in fable and public relations.

Gazing down the Las Vegas Strip with its bright lights, wild architecture, and high-rise megaresorts, it's hard to imagine a time when the only nighttime illumination available was that from the moon.

But the world has discovered Las Vegas. It is a resort destination city, a gambling mecca, an entertainment capital.

It also is a place where approximately one million people live and work and raise their families. Far from a vision of fantasy, the reality of Las Vegas is that it is an enormously prosperous factory town.

Now that you're here, it's time to call it home.

2

Sketching the Vegas Profile

You're a forty-seven-year-old white woman, married, and you own your home. You come from California, have lived in Las Vegas less than five years, and came here for the economic opportunities, tax structure, and mild winters. You've had some college and recently have changed your political party affiliation from Democrat to Republican.

And one more thing.

You are a demographer's dream.

In short, that is the profile of the average Las Vegan: statistically generated, of course, for the booming southern Nevada population is anything but typical.

Fact is, Las Vegas gets a little more gray each year. (This, no doubt, will come as a relief to those of you planning to make it your permanent home.) Poet Robert Browning came up with the ideal Las Vegas motto when he wrote, "Grow old along with me, the best is yet to be," and that appears to apply to southern Nevada as well. At least, statistically.

In 1980, the median age of the typical Las Vegas adult was 40.1 years. Throw in the kids, and the average dipped to 29.7. By 1985, as the valley's senior retirement centers began to catch on with retirees from across the nation, the average age increased to 32.5 with children included. By 1995, the average age of the adult population was 47.

Although the vast majority of southern Nevada's 1 million residents is white, 75.4 percent according to the 1990 U.S. Census, the population remains diverse. One in nine Las Vegans is Hispanic, one in eleven African American, one in thirty Asian. Of all ethnic groups, the Hispanic population has grown the most in the past decade, increasing from 8 percent of the population to 11.2 percent.

Nearly six in ten households have two adults. Almost seven in ten have no children. Although 29 percent of southern Nevadans have maintained residency more than twenty years, more than half the population has been in the valley a decade.

Now comes the staggering part: 7.3 percent of the population, or about one in fourteen southern Nevadans, has lived in Las Vegas less than a year. That's a boomtown by anyone's measure, but at least you need not feel like the only new kid on the block.

Not with the community's expansion and projected growth. In July 1996 alone, 6,620 people made Las Vegas their new residence.

In 1945, about the time Bugsy Siegel got his bright idea to come out to Las Vegas, Clark County's population was 20,000, including jackass prospectors and sand-and-sage cattle ranchers. On the way to surpassing the one million mark, Las Vegas reached the 500,000 mark in the early 1980s, hitting 552,900 by 1985.

That means this diverse population doubled in a decade.

It also has spread out from old and new cities of Henderson (the new Henderson goes by the name Green Valley) on the southeast side of the valley to Mesquite near the Nevada-Utah border. Mesquite, for example, is rapidly transforming itself from a ranching community to one of the hottest casino border towns in the country. Although its population, at just more than 5,500, is tiny by some standards, it represents a 58 percent growth in a single year.

Henderson, once a smoky World War II industrial site, has grown into Nevada's third-largest city with a 1995 population figure of nearly 120,000.

The only spot in southern Nevada that has resisted growth is Boulder City, which emerged during the building of Hoover Dam in the early years of the Great Depression and does not allow casino gambling inside the city limits. With 14,100 residents, and located just fourteen miles from downtown, it is one of the places Las Vegans go to get away from other Las Vegans.

Where are all the people coming from?

California, for starters. A full 42 percent of Las Vegas newcomers hail from the Golden State, which threatened to be renamed the gold-plated state after its oppressive tax structure and early 1990s real estate crash sent thousands fleeing to other states. Southern Nevada also is home to equal measures of New Yorkers and Texans, who some locals believe serve to cancel each other out. Actually, 17 percent of newcomers arrive from the Northeast and Southwest. Another 9.5 percent come from the Midwest, 9 percent from the South. Just more than 5 percent of new residents are from the Northwest.

The state-by-state breakdown, according to the Department of Motor Vehicles, goes something like this: California, Arizona, New York, Texas, Florida, Illinois, Colorado, Utah, Michigan, and Washington.

Nearly three of four southern Nevadans are registered to vote. Traditionally, a majority of the valley's residents was a registered Democrat. That has changed in recent years. In 1995, 42.6 percent of those registered had done so as Republicans, slightly more than the 39.1 percent of registered Democrats. Both Nevada's senators, Harry Reid and Richard Bryan, are Democrats, and as of Election Year 1998, both of the state's members of the House of Representatives, Barbara Vucanovich and John Ensign, were Republicans.

More than other states, Nevada's political history is decidedly Libertarian and, some would argue, libertine as well. More than 18 percent of registered voters consider themselves Independent or members of a less traditional political party.

Once you have begun to comprehend the rate of growth, it's a little easier to appreciate the challenges faced by community planners who went to sleep in a bustling desert outpost and awoke in America's last great boomtown. It might not keep your automobile from overheating while you're sweating out a rush-hour traffic jam or keep you from overheating while waiting for hours to change your license plates at the Department of Motor Vehicles, but at least you can understand what all the commotion is about.

By 1998, the valley's population had risen to 1.3 million, making Clark County the third fastest- growing county in the nation. And they continued to migrate by the thousands each month. According to state demographic experts, at the current rate of expansion — some 5,000 people per month moving to Las Vegas is expected to continue. By 2018, more than 2.7 million people will be crowded into the Las Vegas valley.

The December 1998 jobless rate, at 3.1 percent, was the lowest in 41 years. Not since 1957 had the state's unemployment rate been as low. In all, 46,500 new jobs were produced, thanks mostly to the opening of the Bellagio and the construction of other megaresorts in Las Vegas. Once you've moved to Las Vegas, you soon realize that the city is the economic engine that drives the state.

On the downside, Las Vegans smoke, drink, and, not surprisingly, gamble more than citizens in other cities. The suicide rate is nearly twice the national average. It is a city of great promise and great falls. And vocal enemies.

Dr. James Dobson, President and founder of the Focus on the Family nonprofit Christian organization, was a member of the National Gambling Impact Study Commission, which held meetings across America in 1998 to discuss the influence of legalized gambling on society. In a January 1999 letter to his followers, Dobson attacked legalized gaming, and in effect, Las Vegas, as never before.

"But what about the glitz and glamour of Nevada?" Dobson wrote. "If one scratches beneath the veneer of its gambling-induced prosperity, it becomes apparent that a culture sown on greed and the exploitation of human weakness invariably reaps the social whirlwind. Consider these documented facts: When compared with the 49 other states, Nevada ranks first in the nation in suicide, first in divorce, first in high school dropouts, first in homicide against women, at the top in gambling addictions, third in bankruptcies, third in abortion, fourth in rape, fourth in out-of-wedlock births, fourth in alcohol-related deaths, fifth in crime, and sixth in the number of prisoners locked up. It also ranks in the top one-third of the nation in child abuse, and dead-last in voter participation. One-tenth of all Southern Nevadans are alcoholics. And as for the moral climate, the Yellow Pages of Las Vegas lists 136 pages of advertisements for prostitution by its various names. No wonder they call it 'Sin City. "'

There's something else you should know about moving to Las Vegas. You must be sure to bring with you a thick skin. For all its growth and economic prosperity, and the many positive aspects of living in

Southern Nevada, it's likely the name will forever be stigmatized simply as a den of sin and degradation.

Things change so quickly in Las Vegas that Central Telephone of Nevada must publish a telephone directory twice per year. This directory includes simple city maps, information on cultural and recreational activities, and calendars for many civic organizations.

Once you have moved to Las Vegas, you will wonder at what point you get to call yourself a local. After you have changed your auto license plates, you will be difficult to distinguish from the next newcomer. Here's something to remember: only 22 percent of Las Vegas residents were born in the valley. That means most of the people you meet are a lot like you—from somewhere else.

Chances are good there's room for you in southern Nevada even if you don't fit the profile.

3

Getting Around Town

The winding weekend pilgrimage of tourists from Southern California to Las Vegas on Interstate 15 surely is one of the most incredible spectacles in the history of the automobile. Whether you have lived in Las Vegas a generation or an hour, there is something awe inspiring, and a little scary, about the river of headlamps and metal streaking toward Las Vegas at high rates of speed. The river stretches out for miles northbound on I-15 on Friday night, then reverses itself come Sunday morning. Despite all the marketing and expansion that has taken place in the city in recent years, Las Vegas still draws its largest percentage of gamblers from Southern California.

In 1995, 4.28 million automobiles flowed through Yermo Inspection Station in San Bernardino County,

California. The Las Vegas Convention and Visitors Authority uses the annual inspection station figures as a marketing barometer for Southern California. How the city is doing with San Diegans and Los Angelenos is measured in large part by how many vehicles pass the station. In a decade, vehicle traffic along Interstate 15 had increased from 2.68 million automobiles.

With that image in mind, you may ask yourself some superheated summer afternoon, "Why are they all trying to merge into my lane?"

Add to that the 28 million passengers flowing through McCarran International Airport in 1995, and you have the makings of a traffic jam anywhere in the city from tourist traffic alone. In the same year, slightly more than 29 million people visited Las Vegas.

As you can see, all roads lead to Las Vegas.

Like most American cities, Las Vegas has streets brimming with commuters riding one to a vehicle. One of the noticeable improvements in the transportation picture is the continued growth of the Citizens Area Transit bus system. The CAT carries 3.6 million passengers each month. Of course, the single largest percentage of passengers, two of every ten, rides the Strip bus, which has been popular with tourists for decades. The CAT system is still stretching out in a community which offers no park-and-ride program.

If part of your regular commute includes airline travel, it's important to note that McCarran International Airport, one of the busiest airports in the world, offers 800 scheduled flights a day, and the number of passengers using the facility has doubled in the past decade. In 1998, McCarran opened a shiny new D Terminal with 26 new gates. With an 8.8-percent average annual growth rate over the past decade, McCarran is going to need each of those gates as it is projected to become one of the five busiest airports in the United States not long after the turn of the century.

But most of you will spend a great deal of time in your cars on the roadways. As with most American cities, the largest traffic volumes are recorded during the morning and evening rush hours.

According to a UNLV study, peak hours on city streets generally correspond to 7 AM to 9 AM and 4 PM to 6 pm. McCarran Airport and Las Vegas Boulevard are always busy.

A 1998 UNLV traffic study concluded: "Infrastructure solutions will require improvements for both the tourist and local resident populations that visit and live in the Las Vegas valley. The lack of infrastructure will constrain the number of tourists who can travel to Las Vegas. This will undermine the success of the gaming industry as the supply of new resort hotels and casinos (Bellagio, Paris, Venetian, and Mandalay Bay) continues to increase. Also, the increasing congestion on local arterial and collector streets will degrade the quality of life experienced by local residents. This in turn will have a negative effect on the image of the Las Vegas Valley and its ability to attract new residents."

Meanwhile, transportation departments at the various governmental entities continue to scramble to catch up.

At times it *can* seem as if each one of those roads is jammed bumper to bumper with seething drivers attempting to merge into your lane.

How you perceive southern Nevada's traffic and transportation issues once largely depended on where you came from. Those harried Los Angelenos like to scoff at locals who complain about expressway grid-lock and the seemingly never-ending road projects that have become regular occurrences in Las Vegas. Newcomers from, say, Boise are more likely to grouse that the daily traffic tie-ups, especially during the sweltering summer months, are almost too much to bear.

Today, all southern Nevadans have at least one thing in common. It's the traffic. With as many as 6,000 new residents per month, the streets of Las Vegas have been overwhelmed by automobiles. Commutes that only a few years ago took a matter of minutes to complete now take a half hour and longer.

Hold this truth close to your city map, windshield shade, and "I'm a local, what's it to ya?" bumper sticker: There will be no getting around the city's increasingly twisted traffic problems for the next several years. Help is on the way, but your Yugo is likely to turn 100,000 miles before all the lofty plans to relieve traffic congestion are set in asphalt.

How much traffic you feel you can endure will have a direct impact on where you purchase a home in the valley. Some of the spiffiest new neighborhoods in the far reaches of the valley are still only ten miles from the downtown business district, but are up to forty-five minutes away during rush hour. A ninety-minute daily commute might not make veterans of the Santa Ana Freeway break out in a cold sweat, but, given a five-day workweek, it is nearly two whole days a year spent huffing diesel fumes and listening to inane radio talkshow hosts.

Most knowledgeable students of the valley's traffic woes will tell you they were flat overwhelmed by the crush of automobiles. Extensive studies are ongoing. But here's how far off a previous Nevada Department of Transportation study was: In 1975, the agency predicted that by 1995 48,500 vehicles would use a stretch of asphalt on U.S. 95 between Valley View and Rancho Drive. By 1995, they had missed their prediction by nearly 100,000 automobiles. For the record, traffic is expected to increase from 1.02 million trips per day in 1995 to 1.79 million trips in 2015. Locals just hope the prediction isn't off by a factor of three.

From the most optimistic commuter to the most cynical cabdriver, and all the experts in between, no one anticipates traffic congestion easing in southern Nevada any time soon despite the millions of dollars in improvements underway.

A few of the changes under consideration:

- Installing traffic signals at the on-ramps to U.S. 95.
- Converting U.S. 95 into a double-deck freeway with a four-lane connector to Interstate 15.
- Widening U.S. 95 from the north end of the valley to Interstate 15, which would force dozens of residents to lose their homes.

Meanwhile, plans for the multimillion-dollar Las Vegas beltway continue to be redrafted. With funds allocated, the beltway will slowly but surely make its way around the city. Some politicians feel it is planned too far west to be helpful to commuters who live in many of the west and northwest areas of town.

The Nevada Department of Transportation is willing to listen to your ideas. Visit their office at 7551 Sauer Drive, near the Rainbow Library at the corner of Buffalo and Cheyenne. But start early in case you get stuck in traffic.

With a rapidly increasing traffic flow and daily tie-ups commonplace, sometimes it must seem as if Las Vegans can't get there from here. But they can, and the average commute to work in southern Nevada is 20.4 minutes, about two minutes longer than the 1990 national average, according to the United States Census.

How will you get from point A to point B? By the shortest route possible, of course. Several options are available for those wishing to battle the urban sprawl.

CAT Bus

The Citizens Area Transit (CAT) bus system offers approximately forty routes throughout the Las Vegas valley and operates twenty hours each day. The Downtown Transportation Center is the transfer point for all CAT buses. Buses run every fifteen minutes for busy routes, every thirty minutes in peak hours, and every sixty minutes in nonpeak hours.

Fares are: $1 for adults; $1.50 for the Strip route;

$.50 for youths, seniors, and persons with disabilities; and free for children under five years old. Ask your bus driver for a free transfer, if you will need one, at the time you pay your fare. Monthly passes are also available.

CAT buses are accessible to people in wheelchairs and those needing help reaching the first step. Free certified personal-care attendants are available for customers with disabilities.

For more information on the CAT bus system, call 228-7433.

Taxis

A dozen taxi companies operate in Las Vegas under the administration of the Taxi Cab Authority. All taxis charge the same fare.

With so many Vegas visitor calls on the Strip and downtown, it often is difficult to get a taxi to your home if you live too far outside the tourist areas of town. Taxi drivers prefer to stay near the easy-money areas, including McCarran International Airport. The only taxi companies that take credit cards (American Express only) are Yellow Cab, Checker Cab, and Star Cab.

Trolleys

The city operates eight trolleys on the Strip, from the Sahara Hotel to the Luxor Hotel. They run every twenty minutes and make stops at the front door of each major hotel on the route. The Strip fare is $1.20, and you must have exact change.

Another trolley runs from the Downtown Transportation Center through downtown, to a supermarket and shopping center, and to the Howard Cannon Senior Center. This trolley is available Monday through Friday, 9 A.M. to 5 P.M. at twenty-minute intervals.

The last trolley line is the Meadows Mall express trolley, which runs Monday through Saturday, 10:30 A.M. to 5 P.M. This trolley is a convenient way for people working downtown to go shopping on their lunch hour without having to worry about parking or driving.

Becoming Street Legal

When you move to Nevada, your out-of-state license can only be used for thirty days. You will need to go to one of the full-service branches of the Nevada Department of Motor Vehicles and Public Safety (DMV) to obtain a new license and register your vehicle.

To obtain your Nevada driver's license, you will need to bring proof of your name and age (birth certificate, out-of-state driver's license or passport) and proof of your Social Security number (Social Security card or payroll slip). You must pass a written test based on the driving laws of the state of Nevada. You can obtain a booklet at the DMV entitled, "Nevada Driver's Handbook," which covers all the information on the written test. There is a fee of $20.50 for a driver's license, which will be good for four years.

To register your vehicle in Nevada, you must have the following:

- Nevada Emission Control Certificate;
- Proof of liability insurance on the vehicle;
- Your current registration certificate;
- Verification of vehicle identification (which will be issued to you when your vehicle is inspected);
- Your out-of-state license plates.

To obtain a Nevada Emission Control Certificate, you must go to an authorized service station (on just about every corner) and ask for a smog test. Prices vary, so it pays to shop around before you choose a station. Your vehicle will be connected to a machine and a reading taken. If the vehicle passes, you will be issued a Nevada Emission Control Certificate. If the vehicle does not pass, you will be required to make repairs to your vehicle until it will pass the test.

Your vehicle must have liability insurance, and Nevada's insurance rates are among the highest in the country. Premiums will vary incredibly, so be sure to check around. Your rates will be best, of course, if you have no accidents or tickets on your record.

Your vehicle will be inspected for safety. They will check the lights, turn signals, horn, seat belts, speedometer, and muffler. Also be sure you have a gas cap on your gas tank.

The worst part of registration is the fee. The newer and more expensive your vehicle is, the more it will cost to register. Call the DMV for information.

Once you're street legal, you can join the thousands of other commuters who manage to navigate the streets of the boomtown each day without incident. As for improving the asphalt infrastructure, try to remain patient, and remember help is on the way.

Unfortunately, it might be stuck in traffic.

4

Settling In

Not long after the tracks of William Clark's railroad crossed the valley, Las Vegas faced its first housing crisis. For visitors, accommodations were limited to a cramped room at Ladd's Hotel, where for one dollar travelers bought eight hours of sleep. But they were mistaken if they thought they also received privacy. Alas, room was so scarce, the beds had to be shared.

In those days, people planning to make a home in Las Vegas had to build their own. A lot has changed in ninety years.

Today, the Las Vegas valley is quickly filling up with scores of housing, condominium, and apartment developments. But, with thousands of people moving to the city each month, there still is a housing shortage. The traditional availability of large sections of raw desert real estate has proved one of the saving graces in the southern Nevada home market. Although developments have wreaked havoc with the endangered desert tortoise, they have been able to keep up with the growing demand for houses and apartments. Favorable interest rates have been a boon to the already booming market, and homebuyers have been known to camp out overnight at sales offices to take full advantage of developments in the more popular sections of the valley.

In 1995, the average price of a home in Las Vegas was $130,000. In July 1996, 1,594 new homes were sold and another 1,628 existing homes were resold. Those numbers compare favorably to cities three times the size of Las Vegas. If that sounds outrageous, remember that southern Nevada became home to 6,620 new residents in July alone. With an unemployment rate around 5.25 percent, and several years of growth still expected, it's no wonder the valley has become a magnet for people seeking second chances.

Summerlin, the planned community that sweeps up to the foothills of the Spring Mountain range in the northwest section of the valley, has emerged as a perennial leader in housing sales and development. Developed by the Howard Hughes Corp., Summerlin in 1998 was ranked as the best-selling master-planned community in the United States by Robert Charles Lesser & Co. with 2,881 home sales. That's up 17 percent over the previous year.

In September 1988, the median price of a new home was $136,600, according to Home Builders Research Inc. That's an 8 percent increase over the previous year. But that doesn't mean those selling homes were having a party. With 20,000 new homes expected to be built in 1998, resale prices are some of the poorest in the country. Existing home prices rose a mere 2.2 percent in the year ending in September 1998. That's the second worst percentage in the nation, ahead of only Hawaii. California led the nation with the average value of an existing home jumping 8.5 percent.

Southern Nevada continues to attract apartment development, but the signs are the boom in this market might be coming to an end. With more than 40,000 units built in the 1990s, there is a temporary glut. Monthly rates average $687, a slight decrease from 1997, when more than 10,000 units were built.

Las Vegas appears to have an abundance of all levels of housing — accept the affordable kind as defined by the federal government. Demand far outstrips supply in this area.

To quote a 1998 UNLV housing study: "Affordable housing will continue to be a significant issue for Clark County as the area's population continues to grow. Housing costs in the Las Vegas valley continue to rise faster than increases in household income."

It is important to note that prices for homes of similar square footage and quality vary widely depending on location. In the popular northwest section of the valley, a three-bedroom, two-bath home can be purchased for approximately $120,000. Across the line dividing Las Vegas from North Las Vegas, only a couple miles from the heart of the northwest expansion, the price of a similar home is about $100,000. Further east, the price continues to drop into the $90,000 range.

Why the difference?

North Las Vegas has a largely undeserved reputation as a city stricken by a high crime rate. It is, in fact, no less safe than most Las Vegas neighborhoods. But it is a working-class town with a well-worn midsection, a fact which led city leaders to push for the release of thousands of acres of raw real estate closer to the northwest side from the Bureau of Land Management. The real estate was purchased by local developers, who have created something akin to the New North Las Vegas.

Green Valley in the southeastern end of southern Nevada is a prime example of well-planned growth in a development boom largely ruled by chaos. Its thoroughfares are wide, its developments lined with grass and trees. Commercial development is generally more tightly controlled than in other parts of the valley, and in a valley lacking in parks and community cultural activities, Green Valley is a success story. With increased freeway access, and the potential for the community-wide beltway to pass nearby, it also makes increasing sense for commuters.

Although your first inclination is likely to be to search for a home in one of the sparkling new neighborhoods that seem to pop up daily, many of the best buys are found in the more established areas. You also get the benefit of mature trees and shrubs, and you will be able to enjoy the quality of life in a neighborhood free of that cookie-cutter feel.

Keep in mind your lifestyle, and make sure that what you need is close by. Las Vegas continues to suffer from a shortage of elementary, middle, and high schools. Find out where the nearest schools, hospitals, doctors, and shopping centers are, and most importantly, how far this home is from where you plan to work.

Now, a strong warning about homeowners associations. They are quite common in the newer neighborhoods, especially in the planned communities of Green Valley, Spring Valley, Summerlin, Desert Shores, and Peccole Ranch. To be sure, living in a tightly controlled community has its advantages—the intricate list of Covenants, Conditions, and Restrictions has the effect of keeping neighborhoods uniform and maintaining property values. But the CC&Rs also are a good way to have other people mind your business. They were designed to ensure uniformity and tranquillity in neighborhoods, but the rules often result in Orwellian living conditions.

Liens are put on homes for downright silly code violations such as leaving your garage door open more than a foot; painting your house trim the wrong shade of an approved color; having a satellite dish; putting up a basketball stand; nonregulation shrubbery. One poor soul was harassed for daring to hang an American flag in his front yard.

Association fees are also something to consider when buying in the newer, planned neighborhoods.

Unlike your mortgage payment, association fees never go away and range anywhere from $20 to more than $200 per month depending on the neighborhood. And if you happen to get behind in your payment of association fees, the association has the legal right to put a lien on your home for any unpaid fees and proceed toward auctioning your home to the highest bidder.

If you're renting, you will be faced with the reality that the apartment market in Las Vegas is fast becoming an expensive way to go. Even studio and one-bedroom apartments rent for more than $500 a month in some areas, and the average price for a two-bedroom place continues to climb to more than $600. Given the low interest rates of the mid-1990s, a monthly mortgage payment for an $80,000 starter home was no more than the price of renting a two-bedroom apartment.

There are approximately 150,000 apartment units in the Las Vegas area. Discounts for seniors, military, and casino workers can be found in some apartments. Since Las Vegas has no rent-control laws, and demand is at a premium, rent hikes are common.

Garbage collection and water fees are included in the rental price at most complexes. Most apartment-leasing companies require a six-month or one-year lease along with a security deposit of approximately $175. Expect to complete an application and credit report. If you are not employed, expect to show a bank statement to prove you will be able to pay the rent during the time of the lease.

If you rent a home, the usual procedure is to pay the first and last months' rent plus a security deposit —usually about $2,000 total. Be careful reading the contract—some owners are dishonest and may be able to retain your security deposit for no other reason than that they wish to. Make sure the contract explains exactly how your security deposit will be accounted for.

If you plan to purchase or rent a mobile home, a helpful publication is the free pamphlet *Mobile Home Finder* found in entryways in many grocery stores.

Landscaping

Las Vegas's dry climate and shortage of water are two good reasons to consider a desert landscape for your home. The Las Vegas Valley Water District provides workshops for residents interested in desert landscaping. They are held at the Demonstration Gardens, 3701 West Alta Drive. You will see many plants that will thrive in arid and hot conditions. Call 258-3205 for information about times.

Very important to serious Las Vegas gardeners is a drip irrigation system, which delivers water directly to the roots of trees and eliminates most of the evaporation associated with sprinklers. See your local nursery for materials and advice on drip irrigation systems.

Utilities

You will need to contact utility companies to turn on service for your new home, apartment, or mobile home.

Water

Las Vegas Valley Water District
1001 S. Valley View Boulevard
Las Vegas, NV 89153
870-4194

Homeowners and renters are required to pay a $100 deposit or present a letter of reference from their previous water company stating that all water bills were paid when due for one year. When you apply for service, ask the representative if they are sending out water conservation showerhead kits free of charge. The kit contains showerheads and aerators that will reduce water consumption and thus your water bill.

Electric

Nevada Power Company
6226 W. Sahara Avenue
Las Vegas, NV 89102
367-5555

No deposit is required for a homeowner. Renters should have a letter of reference from their previous electric company stating all electric bills were paid when due for one year or pay a small deposit. There is a $15 connection fee.

Gas

Southwest Gas Corporation
4300 W. Tropicana Avenue
Las Vegas, NV 89103
365-1555

No deposit is required for a homeowner, and you must show proof of ownership. There will be a connection fee of approximately $20.

Southern Nevada's Senior Weatherization program is a free service designed to help homeowners (including owners of mobile homes) conserve energy and lower utility bills. The senior must be at least fifty-five years old, with an annual income of $22,000 or less. The program is available October through May. Volunteer senior energy consultants will visit your home and offer conservation recommendations. Included in the visit is a selection of free weatherization materials installed by the volunteers.

Southwest Gas will also provide you with information you need to find a reputable contractor to replace or repair your heating system.

Sewer

Clark County Sanitation
5857 E. Flamingo Road
Las Vegas, NV 89122
458-1180

Sewer service costs approximately $45 quarterly. No deposit is required.

Trash Removal

Silver State Disposal Service
770 E. Sahara Avenue
Las Vegas, NV 89104
735-5151

Trash pickup takes place twice a week at a cost of approximately $28 quarterly. No deposit is required. Recycling is included in trash removal and takes place on its own calendar. Ask Silver State for your free recycling bins.

Telephone

Sprint/Central Telephone
330 S. Valley View Boulevard
Las Vegas, NV 89153
244-7400

Basic telephone service will cost approximately $12 per month, plus a one-time connection fee of $36.60. Depending on your credit history, there may be a deposit required. (By the way, the statewide area code is 702.)

5

Job Search

Contrary to popular legend, not everyone in Las Vegas deals blackjack for a living. Although casino employees make up a sizable percentage of the employment picture, and are part of a colorful sub-culture, there are more construction workers than card dealers in southern Nevada.

With 30 million visitors a year, Las Vegas is a service-based, tourism-driven economy with all that that implies. Compared to other regions, jobs are plentiful here but traditionally have not paid as well as work requiring more education and training.

A UNLV study released in 1998 put it this way: "As Las Vegas continues to encourage both commercial and residential development, job growth will continue to be concentrated in these lower paying service industry jobs (gaming and construction). Furthermore, when designing an effective growth strategy, the Las Vegas metropolitan area will need to ensure that it has a well trained labor force for the future."

That labor force continues to expand at a staggering rate. The latest available statistics note that 548,300 people are employed in Las Vegas with an average annual wage of $27,709.

The face of the Las Vegas Valley is aging gracefully. State officials project a continued migration of seniors to the warm climate and friendly tax structure of Southern Nevada A 1996 study conducted by the Center for Applied Research bears that out. The study showed seniors are moving here the climate (46 percent), lower taxes (43 percent) and retirement (40 percent).

As the competition for stable employees has increased, the pay scale has improved. Nevada was a national leader in income growth in 1994 and 1995. Through the second quarter of 1996, Nevada remained the country's leader in work creation with 56,000 new jobs in the previous twelve months. Las Vegas, first the previous year, dropped to fifth best in the nation, according to Arizona State's Blue Chip Job Growth Update. The job growth brought the state's total number to 847,000.

Naturally, many of those gains came in the construction industry, which grew by 17.9 percent. But every category saw an increase.

Nevada also is a right-to-work state, which means employees can be fired at the will of the boss. For no reason, but not for a bad reason. After a multimillion-dollar settlement by Hilton Hotels, the heavily lobbied state legislature severely limited punitive damage awards in cases of wrongful termination.

It is important to generate job leads before moving to Las Vegas. Even in a boomtown, the world is a pretty cold place when you are out of work. The longstanding cliché of the carefree new resident who dashes into a casino and lands a high-paying job as a blackjack dealer is largely the stuff of fiction. In today's Las Vegas, even the card dealers must undergo training and background checks—including drug-testing at many resorts—before ever getting near the casino floor.

The best casino jobs at the best resorts are coveted positions that people often work many years to attain. Not only do they pay well, but there is a philosophical shift at many casinos when it comes to employee relations. In the past, the unwritten motto went something like this: "Dummy up and deal." Today, a prospective employee is likely to be required to fill out a job application, as well as undergo an oral and written test. Prior to the opening of the MGM Grand Hotel, prospective employees not only had to complete the paperwork, but they also were asked to sing and dance as if trying out for a chorus line. Old timers scoffed at that, but Grand executives succeeded in finding not only the friendliest workers available, but a few good singers as well.

Here is a Vegas reality for women. If you want to work as a cocktail waitress, you will be forced to wear what, at many resorts, amounts to little more than a bikini, a swatch of fabric, and high heels. Although the jobs pay well when tips are considered, they are not for the faint of heart—or the overweight, middle-aged, or pregnant. The job is one of the bastions of male chauvinism in the casino industry. Although a few cocktail waiters exist, they are not required to wear bikini briefs and a smile.

In southern Nevada, there are forty-six companies with 1,000 or more employees. The largest of these, of course, are casino corporations. Mirage Resorts, for example, employs more than 18,000 workers. In Clark County, approximately 50 percent of workers are employed in service-oriented positions. With so many people in service jobs, it makes sense that there would be fewer working in professional positions. Sure enough, professional people make up only 13 percent of the total work force, compared to 16.6 percent for the rest of the nation.

The median income per Las Vegas household in 1994 was $35,895, substantially higher than the national average.

Although approximately 35,000 casino employees are represented by the Hotel Employees and Restaurant Employees International Union, better known as the Culinary Union, wages and working conditions vary substantially from one resort to another.

The average hourly wage for a blackjack dealer is $4.52, but that number is deceiving. Casino employees make a substantial part of their pay from tips. It is not uncommon for blackjack dealers at Strip hotels to receive more than $100 a day in tips. Add to that the $36.16 daily wage and you have a respectable day's pay.

Here are a few average hourly wages for traditional jobs in the hotel/casino industry: Bartender, $10.77; cashier, $9.03; change person, $7.72; cook, $11.57; food prep, $10.32; front desk clerk, $9.91; housekeeper, $10.28; maid, $8.75; slot mechanic, $13.15; taxicab driver, $5.22 (plus tips); waiter or waitress, $6.86 (tips not included).

Wage rates for private sector positions outside the service industry vary even more dramatically. Here are a few hourly averages: Accountant, $14.18; carpenter, $19.29; cashier, $8.35; cook, $10.90; electrician, $16.00; general office clerk, $8.50; janitor, $8.72; nonunion painter, $14.09; security guard, $8.35; bank teller, $7.95.

The average hourly rate by industry provides a general rule of thumb for what you can expect to earn. Construction, $17.68; manufacturing, $12.72; public utilities, $19.64; retail sales, $8.83; wholesale sales, $13.35.

Dividing the employment pie in Clark County looks something like this: gaming industry, 28 percent; trade, 20 percent; service, 19 percent; government, 11 percent; construction, 8 percent; financial, 5 percent; manufacturing, 4 percent; transportation, 3 percent; public utilities, 2 percent.

All gaming industry workers must obtain a sheriff's card, which has long been one of the "Catch-22s" of the southern Nevada bureaucracy. You need a sheriff's card to work in a casino, but you need a job in a casino before obtaining a sheriff's card. New workers must obtain a referral from their employer before making the trip to 601 East Fremont for the card. The cost is $20 cash, and the card is good for three years. Bring two forms of identification. Also keep in mind that many Nevada employers require preemployment drug testing.

Then there is the Techniques of Alcohol Management card, or TAM card. In Nevada, all workers who serve, sell, or come in contact with alcohol must obtain a TAM card. Here's how to get one: attend a four-hour class, pass an easy test, and pay $18. The card is good for five years. The office is located at 557 East Sahara Avenue, Suite 223.

To work as a food handler or in child care, you must obtain a health card. The health district will give you a TB test and a two-hour class. The cost is $10 for the certificate, which you can obtain prior to being hired. The Clark County Health District is located at 625 Shadow Lane.

As of July 1996, the federal minimum wage was $4.25, but there are a few exceptions to the rule in Nevada. For teenagers under eighteen, the figure is $3.23. Eighteen to twenty-one, it is $3.80. State law does not allow employers to count tips against the minimum wage.

Unemployment dipped to 5.6 percent in southern Nevada in 1995—the lowest rate in many years. In January 1996, there were 616,300 people in the work force, approximately 33,000 of them looking for jobs.

Although the city is known as a national leader in job production, unemployment is still a factor. The average unemployment-insurance check a worker receives is $183.85 per week, with a twenty-six-week maximum. The most a worker can receive is $237. The Nevada Employment Security Department (486-3300) provides the most basic of job services for southern Nevada residents. The NESD uses a computerized job bank to assist in placing workers. Nevada Business Services (384-7655) is a nonprofit organization that provides training and leads for economically disadvantaged residents.

The Yellow Pages are riddled with employment services, the best of which offer assistance at no cost to the worker. Also the local newspapers have large parts of the classified section devoted to employment opportunities. Some of the jobs are not ideal, but they are a good place to start.

The *Las Vegas Review-Journal* publishes several pages of employment opportunities. New hotel-casinos, homes, shopping centers, and industrial complexes are being built every year, so the job outlook remains high. The availability of work is one of the advantages of living in a boomtown.

6

Boomtown Education

Clark County faces a crisis in education that cannot be understated. The economic prosperity that has attracted thousands to the desert has overwhelmed the Clark County School District's educational infrastructure. With the growth of the nineties, Las Vegas became a great place for teachers to find work, but an increasingly harsh place for students to find a quality education.

That's not the fault of the school district administration, headed by schools' Superintendent Dr. Brian Cram. The simple fact is, the valley has reached the point where it has barely enough seats for its students. As a result, national test scores are lower than average, a crisis in special education exists, students are forced to attend schools on double sessions (one morning school and one afternoon school in the same building). Even simple textbooks are hard to find at some schools.

It is clear that all of southern Nevada's economic success has been toughest on its children. Nevada has the highest teen suicide rate and the second highest teen pregnancy rate in the nation. Its dropout rate is at the top year after year. (It was 11.7 percent in 1994.) Its teen death rate is fourth highest, and it has the highest teen incarceration rate.

While growth and the Las Vegas lifestyle are contributing factors, Nevada's traditional political philosophy also plays a role. The same low tax rates and libertarian bent that attracts so many to the state reveals itself at the bottom line when it comes to paying for, for instance, aid to preschool children. Nevada ranks last.

In an attempt to resolve the crisis, community leaders have lobbied hard for the voter passage of multimillion-dollar bond issues to build new elementary, middle, and high schools as fast as they can be constructed. Dozens of new teachers are hired before the start of each school year, and Cram and his administration continue to look at new ways to treat special-needs students.

"Education is about opening doors," Cram told leaders from the political, business, and education communities. "It's not about closing cell doors behind some teenager. It's not about closing the classroom door to some young mother. It's about opening doors."

Cram has done his homework, but he has a Herculean job on his hands.

Public Elementary and Secondary Schools

Clark County has the nation's tenth largest school district. In the mid-1990s, it had 184 schools and approximately 175,000 students. There are 25 high schools, including the Southern Nevada Vocational Technical Center; 27 middle schools; 127 elementary schools; and 5 schools for handicapped children. (The school district headquarters is located at 2832 East Flamingo Road. Phone number: 799-5011.)

Many elementary schools are on a year-round schedule to accommodate the large number of students. Seven middle schools also have a year-round schedule, which in many instances is a different schedule than elementary schools. Try planning a vacation around those conflicting schedules, and you'll be ready for a job with the school district.

For the most part, the high schools remain on traditional nine-month schedules. Check with the school district for more information on particular schools. A dozen schools were scheduled to be built during the 1996–1997 school year.

Students must be five years old on or before September 30 to enter kindergarten and six years old on or before September 30 to begin first grade. Kindergarten is not compulsory.

To register your child, you must bring a certified birth certificate, up-to-date immunization records, two proofs of address (utility bill and rent receipt, for example), and the name and address of the previous school attended, if any. The Clark County Health Department, 625 Shadow Lane, Las Vegas, NV 89127, offers free immunizations.

Parents may choose to have their children apply to one of several so-called "magnet" middle schools and high schools. These schools specialize in various areas of study not offered at the standard schools. Magnet schools allow students to choose educational experiences based on their interests.

In addition to its high dropout rate, Nevada ranks last among states in sending students to college. The national average for students attending some college is 53.5 percent. In Nevada, the rate is only 32.8 percent.

For adults needing to complete their high school education, several alternative schools are available, offering classes with flexible hours to fit your work schedule. Contact your school district for more information.

Private schools must be licensed by the Nevada State Department of Education. Many such private schools are affiliated with churches. All are listed in the local telephone directory.

Community College of Southern Nevada

If Las Vegas faces a crisis in elementary education, its community college system is progressing nicely. Although crowded, it continues to successfully pursue its mission: to provide affordable, practical course work for adults with short-term and long-range educational goals. Las Vegas is also home to

Community College of Southern Nevada. CCSN's dental hygiene program is rated number two in America. The culinary program is ranked third. The community college also has nursing and theater programs, and the variety of courses offered range from sports betting and the basics of electricity to English composition and Nevada history.

Three campuses allow students from each side of town convenient access to classes. The main campus is on East Cheyenne Avenue in North Las Vegas. There is a campus on West Charleston Boulevard, on the west side of town; and the third campus is in Henderson.

CCSN offers many programs designed to keep people involved in education. GED preparation courses help students sharpen skills in math, reading, and writing before taking the high school equivalency test. The "first course free" program helps Nevada high school graduates who have never attended college.

Also available is the Silver Sage College program for seniors, making CCSN classes free of charge for seniors over sixty-two years old. In addition to traditional financial aid programs, veterans may be eligible for Veterans' Administration education benefits. Students with disabilities can take advantage of special counseling and other services provided by Access to Community College Educational Support Services (ACCESS).

The CCSN Planetarium presents wonderful movies in a 360-degree dome. After the last performance, weather permitting, telescope viewing is available.

University of Nevada, Las Vegas

Newcomers to Southern Nevada probably know the University of Nevada, Las Vegas, from its reputation as a college basketball powerhouse. But it's more than that. It also is one of the nation's fastest-growing state universities—and one of the youngest. The growing pains are evident in crowded classrooms and difficult course scheduling, but the university under President Carole Harter appears to be adjusting to the infrastructural stresses.

UNLV offers nearly 140 undergraduate, master's, and doctoral degree programs from eleven colleges and two schools. All UNLV programs are accredited by the Northwest Association of Schools and Colleges.

The university operates on a semester calendar, with two semesters of approximately sixteen weeks each, plus a summer session from May through August. Application deadlines are July 15 for fall semester and December 15 for spring semester. Students must be fully immunized prior to registering for classes. Contact the Student Health Center for more information at 895-3370.

Residence and dining halls are available for students wishing to live in campus. Numerous financial aid programs are also available to students, including grants, loans, scholarships and employment programs.

Its 335-acre campus can be seen by guided tour Monday through Friday through the Office of Admissions (call 895-3443 for an appointment).

Vocational Training

Southern Nevada has to be the center of the universe for private schools offering practical training for working adults. Dozens of occupational schools are available for training in specialized fields such as bartending, dog grooming, truck driving, cosmetology, casino dealing, interior design, floral design, and real estate. For more information, contact the school or the Commission of Postsecondary Education, 1820 East Sahara Avenue #111. Phone number: 486-7330.

7

This is the City

"Las Vegas is a city in statistics only. In every other respect, it is a jungle—a jungle of green-felt crap tables and slot machines in which the entire population, directly or indirectly, is devoted to fleecing tourists. There were 12 million of these in 1962 (17 million in the state), and the number has been increasing each year. They come to gamble or to have a fling or out of curiosity, and Las Vegas embraces them all, eager to satisfy their craving for gambling—or any vice—with a flourish not seen since Cecil B. De Mille's last Roman spectacle."

Kind of scary, isn't it?

That's the way investigative reporters Ed Reid

and Ovid Demaris sized up Las Vegas in their classic 1963 book, *The Green Felt Jungle.*

One peek at the seamy side of Sin City through the eyes of Reid and Demaris and it's a wonder anyone would want to even visit Las Vegas, much less move there. *The Green Felt Jungle* captured the public's fascination with the prurient nature of the city, but it failed to paint a full picture or depict life outside the so-called jungle. With its history of organized crime activity, and by the very nature of the casino business, Las Vegas has developed a dark reputation that persists to this day.

In part, that reputation is deserved, for any place that generates as many billions in cash revenue as Las Vegas is bound to attract an army of scam artists and cheap hoods. That reputation, much like *The Green Felt Jungle,* fails to tell the whole story of life in southern Nevada.

According to state statistics, for every 100,000 Nevadans, there are 870 adults on probation, 326 on parole, and 460 in prison. In the past decade, Nevada's prison population has increased by more than 100 percent. In a nation that incarcerates more of its citizens than any on the planet, Nevada is first in the country in locking up its convicted felons.

"The reality is, crime is going down," Sheriff Jerry Keller told a group of reporters in May 1996. "This is a very safe city, one of the safest of the major cities. . . . This may very well be the safest tourist city in the world."

Ah, there it is. Las Vegas is a safe place—for a

tourist city. With billions flowing through the valley, and more than 30 million visitors each year, southern Nevada never will be looked upon as just another American metropolis with one million residents. Not with some of the state's largest security forces wearing the uniforms not of the Metropolitan Police Department or Nevada Highway Patrol, but the Mirage, Circus Circus, and Hilton.

Just where does Las Vegas rank compared to other cities?

With approximately 7,300 crimes per 100,000 individuals, in 1995 Las Vegas checked in around 100th among the nation's largest cities, according to FBI and Morgan Quitno Press reports.

In the late 1970s, Las Vegas held the dubious distinction of being America's least safe city, but in the past two decades the trend has been more positive. Although the number of crimes committed has risen as the community has grown, the city actually has become statistically safer in many categories. In 1995, there were 60,163 crimes reported from a population of 824,050—not including another 30 million visitors. Rapes and robberies have declined, but the number of homicides—often attributable to the increase in street-gang violence—has continued to rise.

The increase in gang-related activity is part of the price southern Nevada is paying for its growth. In 1995, 506 drive-by shootings were investigated by Metropolitan police. *Money* magazine recently changed Las Vegas's ranking from 5th to 114th on its list of Most Liveable Cities in the United States during that period, in part because of the troubling lifestyle trends, including air quality and criminal activity.

Here again, Nevada's low-tax, libertarian philosophy reveals itself in a distinct lack of police officers per capita (approximately 2 per 1,000 citizens) as compared to other American cities. Although voters pass almost annually bond issues calling for more police officers, the community lags behind in the number of public servants, if not service.

Then there are the quasi-legal business activities that attract attention to the city's eccentric side. Many nude—or partially nude—dancing clubs can be found in Las Vegas. Once they obtain the proper licenses, they are legal businesses that just happen to be hot spots of illegal activity. Prostitution is illegal in Clark County, but you wouldn't know it by reading the Yellow Pages "entertainer" advertisements. Although legal prostitution takes place in neighboring Nye County, which includes Pahrump, the illegal racket flourishes in Las Vegas.

There are also a handful of sex-tease clubs, in which the nude working women inside promise more than they deliver. Tourists are asked to purchase extremely expensive nonalcoholic drinks, presumably to pay for sex. However, after customers spend hundreds of dollars for $3 and $4 bottles of sparkling juice, they are escorted to the door by bouncers who handle complaints their own way. Most customers do not complain to police, since they themselves were attempting to break the law by paying for sex in Clark County.

A UNLV study on the subject concluded the following: "The cities of Las Vegas, North Las Vegas, and Henderson should examine the problems of Florida and not follow in its footsteps. Crime in the Las Vegas valley is on the decline, but is still above the national average. The continued growth of the valley will surely create more instances of crime and place more burdens on the criminal justice system."

*   *   *

What happened to the Bugsy Siegel types, anyway?

Contrary to what some of today's MBA-toting casino operators would have the world believe, organized crime still operates in southern Nevada. According to the FBI, the remnants of the traditional mob can be found in the areas of illegal bookmaking (where they offer credit to players) and high-interest loanshark loans (which often are made to degenerate gamblers and desperate businessmen). But federal law enforcement has placed La Cosa Nostra below violent street gang-related crime and white-collar crime on its priority list.

The days of the mob operating openly in a casino's front office are over, but the shadow of organized crime has managed to survive decades after *The Green Felt Jungle* fell from the bestseller list.

New residents soon discover that, for all its hype and bluster, when it comes to crime, Las Vegas is a big city like any other.

8

Getting the Vegas Idea

Imagine working in a whiskey distillery and insisting on constantly sampling the wares. You would be at best foolish and at worst an unemployed alcoholic.

It's that way in Las Vegas with gambling. It's no shame to take a drink, or in this case, to play the slots or sit at a blackjack table. But it is the worst sort of folly to think that you can gamble regularly and expect to pay your monthly mortgage and utilities, much less put food on the table.

This is not a diatribe against the evils of gambling. Far from it. Las Vegas was built on cards and dice and the wonders of the house edge. It is safe to say there would be no boomtown if it weren't for the gold mines that operate disguised as casino resorts.

With that said, you need to remember one thing when you move to Las Vegas: Gambling is for tourists, not locals.

Every foolproof system for beating the house has one common denominator: a fool behind it all. It is hard to stress this enough. The gambling business has put food on countless tables and sent thousands of kids to college. Gambling has ruined countless lives and shattered families like carnival glass. Working in the industry is one thing; pretending you will get rich as a player is another.

In fact, many casino executives no longer refer to their business as gambling. Because, they privately note, there is no gamble involved. The house edge is too strong. Instead, they prefer to view gamblers as guests who "rent space" at the slot machines and table games.

Even good gamblers bust out. Even the best sports bettors. Even the world's greatest poker players. Even Nick the Greek. Even Jimmy the Greek. If they all fall short occasionally, what reasonable chance do you have?

The answer is, no chance at all.

With that said, it does not mean that if you play a roll of quarters in a video poker machine that you will become some glassy-eyed, slack-jawed zombie forever chasing Lady Luck's petticoat. Hardly. For many people, gambling is fun and entertaining. A sports bet is a great way to maintain interest in an otherwise boring football game. Dropping a bucket of change into a slot machine passes the time and can be a lot of fun—especially if you take advantage of the inexpensive food and drinks casinos offer their customers.

That really is the lesson of this chapter: If you gamble, go for the value and never lose sight of what you are doing. If you gamble, you will lose. Perhaps not the first time, but eventually. If you gamble a little, you will call it entertainment. If you gamble a lot, you will call it the dumbest thing you ever did. Gambling is for tourists and people with money to burn.

All right. The sermon is over. You have listened, contemplated the facts of life inside the casino, and still you want to try your luck.

No one can blame you. It's pretty exciting hitting a jackpot or turning over a card and making 21. So if you're going to gamble, here are a few tips:

First, never play the big wheel in any casino. It's a carnival sucker bet that gives the casino a whopping big percentage of your wager. Stay away from Keno, too. It takes 25 percent of your bet. Shy away from gimmicky card games such as Caribbean poker and red dog unless you want to play for the sheer fun of playing and observing your money do strange things before it is drawn into the casino coffers.

Roulette may be fun to watch, but American roulette, with its "0" and "00" is a game for lollipops. Don't you be one.

Blackjack is an easy game to understand, but a difficult one to beat. Card counting is supposed to be an easy path to riches, but most card counters die broke. The casino has a dozen ways to frustrate card counters. Still, it won't hurt to read a book on black-jack to learn what card counting is all about.

Craps and baccarat give you the best odds for your money and are not difficult to understand. A good book can teach you either game in a matter of a few minutes.

The most savvy book on casino games and the easiest to understand was written by my publisher, Lyle Stuart. Its title is *Winning at Casino Gambling*, and $18 gets you a copy at your local bookshop, or you can order one by mail from Barricade Books, 150 Fifth Avenue, Suite 700, New York, New York 10011.

Most important: Never bet more than you can lose.

Better still, don't bet at all, and you're a sure winner! Gambling is not for working people who plan to live and prosper in the world's largest casino city.

9

Desert Culture

One of the raps on living in Las Vegas is that it is devoid of cultural activity. Ballet companies across America might suffer from a lack of public support and funding, but Las Vegas is bound to be criticized for not being more civilized.

Face it, the city is an easy target. When you promote the world's largest hotels shaped like pyramids, castles, and fantasy lands, and offer topless revues, cheap buffets, and acres of free parking, it's hard to blame people for not appreciating your more polished side.

But the fact is, Las Vegas is growing up. Slowly, to be sure, for its libertarian side is unlikely ever to support taxpayer-funded operas and dance festivals, but

it is maturing just the same. Today, more than ninety not-for-profit arts and cultural organizations are
registered locally. The mother of all arts groups is
the Allied Arts Council, which keeps track of each
organization. (Call 731-5419 for information and list-
ings.) It's not the only clearinghouse for the fine
arts. There also are arts councils in Henderson (458-
8855) and Boulder City (294-5058).

Then come the venues. You won't find the local
ballet troupe performing at the Stardust. Not when
the Cashman Field Theater offers 1,940 seats. The
Government Center Amphitheater downtown has
3,000 seats and is home to popular jazz concerts.
The $2 million Sammy Davis, Jr., Festival Plaza
Amphitheater offers 500 seats and a variety of acts
throughout the year ranging from bluegrass and jazz
to traditional African and Hawaiian music.

The University of Nevada, Las Vegas, on Maryland
Parkway offers a year-round schedule of events and
is highlighted by the Charles Vanda Masters Series
at the 1,885-seat Artemus W. Ham Concert Hall. The
Vanda Masters Series, which attracts the greatest
names in classical music, has been around since
1976—that's ancient history by Las Vegas standards.

In September, Nevada Shakespeare in the Park
performs the Bard's work in Green Valley. The festival draws an average of 25,000 people a year to the
outdoor plays at Foxridge Park.

There are plenty of places to view local theater
and dance, as well as the work of local and regional
artists. While Las Vegas is unlikely ever to rival Chicago,
New York, or other large cities for traditional culture,

it finally is growing into its own.

One of the intriguing aspects of Las Vegas is that most of its best sculptures are not found in museums, but either in public places or in casinos. Most of its wildlife are not located at the diminutive Las Vegas Zoological Park on Rancho Drive, but at the resorts.

You will need a car to discover the culture in southern Nevada.

For statues, Las Vegas must lead all cities its size and age in sheer numbers. In Green Valley, eighteen lifelike sculptures grace the public spaces. Many were commissioned from J. Seward Johnson, Jr., and are easily sighted on Green Valley Parkway near Sunset Road. And there is *Circle of Light* by William Limebrook, located in Summerlin. *Flashlight* by Claes Oldenburg graces the campus of UNLV.

One of the more controversial works of art in the city is *Ground Zero* by William Maxwell. The 280-square-foot wall mural spreads out across City Hall downtown.

No casino offers more sculptures than Caesars Palace, which features marble replicas of *David, The Rape of the Sabines,* and two dozen more pieces not to be seen outside of the Louvre.

The valley offers more than two dozen nonprofit art galleries. A few include the Boulder City Art Gallery, Charleston Heights Arts Center Gallery, Donna Beam Fine Arts Gallery at UNLV, and the Las Vegas Art Museum.

For students of Vegas culture, there's the Debbie Reynolds Hollywood Movie Museum, which features an impressive costume collection and plenty of film clips from Hollywood's Golden Age.

And no local's life in Las Vegas is complete without a trip to the ever-campy Liberace Museum. Any place offering the world's largest rhinestone on display can't be all bad. It also features the world's loudest costumes worn by the late entertainer.

Those preferring more traditional museums will find the Las Vegas Natural History Museum, Nevada State Museum and Historical Society, and the Old Mormon Fort State Historic Park not only quaint but also informative.

The Marjorie Barrick Museum of Natural History at UNLV is free and full of desert animals and Nevada natural history. The Clark County Heritage Museum at Boulder City is home to a "Nevada Home" exhibit as well as railroad cars and the original Boulder City train depot. Don't expect the Smithsonian, but be prepared to gain genuine insight into the colorful heritage of the city and state.

For those who need to get their culture from the airwaves, KNPR (89.5 FM) is the valley's National Public Radio station and offers classical music, news, and commentary. KUNV (91.5 FM) offers jazz all day and alternative rock all night. On the weekends, it features an eclectic schedule ranging from folk and bluegrass programs to shows in Spanish, French, and German. KLVX Channel 10 is the public television station and carries the traditional programs.

Libraries

In the early 1990s, and thanks to the passage of an $80 million bond issue, the Clark County Library District more than doubled. So did the number of private bookstores. With thirteen library branches and eleven rural libraries, the district has more than 473,000 active library-card users. The libraries are run by trained staff and approximately 4,000 volunteers.

Library Director Darrell Batson's philosophy: "Las Vegas is a multiethnic community and the Las Vegas-Clark County Library District has more than 2,000,000 items in languages to meet those needs."

Following the national trend toward specialization and computerization has been a challenge for southern Nevada library officials. They have been criticized for spending too much on fanciful architecture and computers and not enough on books. But the district continues to respond to the criticism and has spent nearly $5 million in recent years on books.

The libraries in Las Vegas are, for the most part, new and beautiful buildings. Each one has its own specialty and character. All are wheelchair-accessible and offer a children's section.

The West Charleston library, in the southwest sector, has the only public medical and health science collection in southern Nevada. It also offers a 289-seat lecture hall.

The Rainbow Library, in the northwest, has an outdoor amphitheater with seating for 500 people and a meeting room for 160 people.

The Summerlin library has a beautiful 291-seat theater which allows community and children's groups to perform in a first-class atmosphere. A conference room, study room, and art gallery are also found here. Because it is a large library, it's a good place to find a quiet spot and read.

The Whitney Library, in Green Valley, has a large Spanish-language collection, 198-seat theater, and a soundproof music practice room.

The largest library, the Clark County Library on East Flamingo Road, has a vast collection of books. It is a good place to go for copies of national and international newspapers.

The West Las Vegas Library has a large 299-seat theater with orchestra pit and dressing rooms.

Perhaps the most interesting library is the Las Vegas Library and Lied Discovery Children's Museum a short distance from downtown. The library offers individual study rooms and the latest in library technology. A word of caution about this library: it is located in an area of town where there is a large homeless population. It's not dangerous, but it can get a bit gamy if you run into library patrons who have not bathed in a few days. Individual study rooms are available.

The Sahara West Library, in the southwest part of town, is a unique building housing a 150-seat multipurpose room, two small conference rooms, an art gallery, and a microcomputer center.

Not all the books in Las Vegas are sports books and not all the culture comes with its top discarded.

10

Child's Play

Despite intensive marketing to families, Las Vegas remains an adult playground for tourists. Now that you have decided to move to Las Vegas, however, you will begin to see the actual community that often is overshadowed by the megaresorts and outdazzled by the neon.

One of the perennial misconceptions about southern Nevada is that it is bereft of things to do for young people. Jokes about sending a Las Vegas kid to dealers school instead of summer camp are as old as vaudeville around these parts. The fact is, although the lifestyle can be hard on families, the community endures and prospers because it continues to evolve into a relatively normal place to raise children—outside the Strip and downtown, that is.

Las Vegas suffers from the usual big-city maladies, and all the stresses that young people face in Boise, Boston, and Baton Rouge apply, but those who simply can't find anything for their progeny to do just aren't looking very hard.

It's probably out of habit, but the first place where parents look for activities for their children is inside the tourist corridor. There, they see that nearly every resort offers a high-tech arcade—Circus Circus, Luxor, Excalibur, and Treasure Island probably feature the best. In addition, Circus Circus has the Grand Slam Canyon Adventure Dome with its double-looping Canyon Blaster roller coaster, the MGM Grand Hotel and Theme Park has the 250-foot Skycoaster and a faux Hollywood backlot. Atop the Stratosphere Tower, there's the Let It Ride High Roller roller coaster and the truly exciting Big Shot space ride. All true, all entertaining.

All the kind of things tourists adore.

But you're not tourists anymore, remember? (You probably will have to remind yourself of that a time or two.)

If you're headed to the Strip, try the Mirage dolphin habitat, where six Atlantic bottlenose dolphins play for the halibut. Or head to Caesars Palace, a resort decidedly not designed with children in mind, and try the Omnimax Theater with its eighty-nine speakers and eighty-nine-foot screen with 360-degree viewing. It's not expensive, and some of the movies are educational as well as entertaining. On Rancho Drive, there's the Santa Fe ice rink, one of two rinks in the valley. A window seat at the Santa Fe Buffet provides a grand view of the rink and is an especially entertaining treat during youth hockey or figure-skating practice.

In the summer, when the 100-plus-degree temperatures are enough to make you have second thoughts about moving to the middle of the Mojave Desert, the Wet 'n' Wild water park on the Strip is a great excuse to cool off. Two tips: Make a day of it by arriving early, and always check the local newspapers for coupons knocking a few bucks off the admission price.

The Imperial Palace is home to more than 750 antique automobiles and motorcycles, including a $50 million collection of Model J Duesenbergs. The collection features automobiles owned by Adolf Hitler (a 1939 Mercedes-Benz 770K) and Elvis Presley (a 1976 Cadillac Eldorado).

If one three-minute ride on a roller coaster possibly can be worth taking a forty-five-minute drive, then the Desperado at Primm on the Nevada-California border is that coaster. At 225-feet high, it's the world's tallest coaster. At a top speed of eighty-miles-per-hour, reaching three Gs in someplaces, it's not for the squeamish. You won't need the address, but it's located at Buffalo Bill's.

So much for the usual suspects.

Once you've settled in, check out one of the valley's twenty-eight community centers for information on recreation classes, crafts, and workshops. The community centers also have after-school programs available. For instance, the Mirabelli Center offers weight lifting and basketball, and the Lowden Center has a children's library. (Children's sections are a part of every library in southern Nevada.)

For the athlete, nine separate Little Leagues blanket southern Nevada, and for special instruction there's the Las Vegas Baseball Academy run by former professional players Mike Martin and Jerry DeSimone. Clark County offers youth basketball leagues for boys and girls age seven to fourteen. There are two bicycle motocross clubs, four amateur boxing gyms, five swim associations, and more than a dozen public pools, four track and field associations, and numerous youth soccer organizations. (The Nevada State Youth Soccer Association telephone number is 594-KICK.)

There's Pop Warner football and amateur gymnastics, and the City of Las Vegas offers outdoor recreation programs for the physically and mentally challenged.

The fact is, there is plenty to keep young people physically and intellectually active and out of harm's way, but, as in any community, it takes dedicated parents to get the ball rolling.

Now, a quick word about the Southern Nevada Zoological Park on North Rancho Drive. It's small. Tiny, in fact. Approximately fifty animals are encamped on a two-acre site with a small petting zoo and the requisite Bengal tiger, chimp, exotic birds, and reptiles. The zoo's administration has been fined for failing to sufficiently care for some animals, but its problem stems as much from a lack of community support as from a lack of animal husbandry. In a city that touts the wildest animal acts this side of Africa, the lack of support for the community zoo is an abomination.

All great cities have great zoos. Visiting the Southern Nevada Zoological Park is a reminder that Las Vegas is painfully young and still has some growing to do.

11

Active Seniors

The secret is out. Las Vegas has become one of the most popular places in America for people of retirement age. With its friendly tax structure and warm, dry climate, the valley continues to draw thousands of seniors each year.

The face of the Las Vegas Valley is aging gracefully. State officials project a continued migration of seniors to the warm climate and friendly tax structure of Southern Nevada A 1996 study conducted by the Center for Applied Research bears that out. The study showed seniors are moving here for climate (46 percent), lower taxes (43 percent) and retirement (40 percent).

Many move into planned communities tailored to their lifestyles such as 1,892-acre Sun City with homes ranging from $85,000 to more than $200,000. Others prefer to buy a condominium or rent an apartment. No matter. Las Vegas has become senior-friendly.

Senior housing developments typically require that at least one person of at least age fifty-five remains in residence. Other adults may live in the home, but anyone nineteen years or younger must be a visitor.

Here are a few senior housing options:

The Villas, 850 homes on the northwest side of town, are adjacent to the Los Prados golf course. Homes are priced from $105,000 to $250,000. Address: 5150 Las Prados Circle. Telephone: 451-6222.

Quail Estates West, 200 homes in the center of the valley, is near Sahara Avenue at 2851 South Valley View Boulevard. Prices begin at $107,000. Telephone: 221-9054.

Promenade at the Meadows, in west Las Vegas near Decatur and Meadows Lane, has homes priced from approximately $150,000 and offers twenty-four-hour security, a clubhouse, and a putting green.

El Paseo, 8078 Kinsella Way, also offers a seniors-only neighborhood with a swimming pool, tennis courts, and a security gate.

Las Vegas also has fourteen retirement apartment communities, many with extra features you would not receive at a regular apartment community, such as housekeepers, meal plans, social activities, shuttle buses, and personal care.

Seniors will want to check in with the local office

of the American Association for Retired Persons. Telephone: 386-8661. The AARP is helpful in getting relocating seniors settled and acquainted with southern Nevada. Another address to remember is 340 North Eleventh Street, location of the Howard Cannon Senior Service Center. In all, southern Nevada offers eighteen senior centers offering field trips, speakers, recreation, and workshops.

UNLV offers classes for seniors sixty-two and over free of charge not including lab fees. Summer classes at UNLV are 50 percent off for seniors. UNLV's Continuing Education program offers courses designed for seniors.

Those newcomers who haven't lost their wanderlust will want to contact Geraldine Wulf at Senior Tripsters. Telephone: 387-0007. Senior Tripsters is an active travel club for older persons. The group organizes brief and extended outings exclusively for seniors.

After you have unpacked and settled in to your new residence, it will be time to exercise. For really active seniors, there's the Nevada Senior Olympics. Telephone: 294-2954. With fifteen events and various age brackets, there's something for everyone.

12

The Right Price

When tourists visit Las Vegas, they rarely leave the Strip or downtown. Now that you're a local, you will want to take advantage of a few of the many things to do outside the sweeping casino districts.

This list is by no means complete, but it makes for a good place to start. Best of all, at little or no cost, each entry is the right price.

Enjoy!

Marjorie Barrick Museum of Natural History: University of Nevada, Las Vegas, 4505 South Maryland Parkway. Telephone: 895-3381. This museum features exhibits of real desert animals, archaeology, anthropology, and history of Nevada and the Southwest. Smithsonian traveling exhibits are also displayed. There is a gift shop and a two-acre garden. Hours: Monday-Friday, 8 A.M. to 4:45 P.M., Saturday, 10 A.M. to 2 P.M.

Cranberry World West: Ocean Spray's Cranberry World West is worth the drive to Henderson. It offers a lighthearted cranberry cinema, interactive media exhibits, plant processing and packaging (where visitors can watch the various processes involved in juice processing and bottling). Each visitor gets a free juice drink. There's also a funky gift shop. 1301 American Pacific Drive. Telephone: 566-7160. Hours: daily, 9 A.M. to 5 P.M.

Enigma Cafe/Poetry Readings: 918-$^1/_2$ South Fourth Street. Telephone: 386-0999. For the price of a good cup of coffee, you can check out poetry readings and folk music in a bohemian setting. Poetry at 7 P.M. on Thursday, music schedule varies.

Boulder City-Hoover Dam Museum: 444 Hotel Plaza, Boulder City. Telephone: 294-1988. Displays historical artifacts related to the construction of Hoover Dam. Watch a free twenty-eight-minute movie entitled, *The Construction of Hoover Dam*. Gift shop. Hours: daily, 10 A.M. to 4 P.M.

Bruno's Indian and Turquoise Museum: 1306 Nevada Highway, Boulder City. Telephone: 293-4865. The odd but interesting display offers a view of the history of turquoise mining and jewelry making. A trading post and gallery are on site. Hours: daily, 9 A.M. to 6 P.M.

Barbara Greenspun Lecture Series: Located at UNLV's Artemus W. Ham Concert Hall, the lecture series is free and features top names from the national news pages. This series is by ticket only on a first-come-first-served basis. Limited to two tickets per person. Call 895-4352 the university for a schedule.

Desert Valley Museum: 31 West Mesquite Boulevard, Las Vegas. This museum displays pioneer vintage quilts, wedding dresses, and more. Hours, Monday–Saturday, 8 A.M. to 5 P.M.

Las Vegas Art Museum: 6132 West Charleston Boulevard. Telephone: 259-4458. The exhibits in the museum's three galleries change monthly. Excellent collection of work from local artists. The museum's store sells art at reasonable prices. Hours: Tuesday–Saturday, 10 A.M. to 3 P.M., Sunday, noon to 3 P.M.

Barrick Lecture Series: Located at UNLV's Artemus W. Ham Concert Hall, this free lecture series is a local favorite and has attracted guests ranging from President Jimmy Carter to Henry Kissinger. Box office telephone: 895-3801. Tickets are available on a first-come-first-served basis, with a limit of two tickets per person.

Bonnie Springs Ranch Petting Zoo: Bonnie Springs Ranch Road, Old Nevada. Telephone: 875-4300. Located near Red Rock Canyon, the petting zoo features usual and unusual farm animals. A restaurant and barbecue area is available. Hours: daily, 10:30 A.M. to 5 P.M.

Las Vegas-Clark County Library District Film Series: Shown at most branches throughout the year. Free admission. Call your local branch.

UNLV International Film Series: University of Nevada, Las Vegas. Programmed by Dr. Hart Wegner, director of film studies at UNLV, the series features a compelling list of international art cinema. Hours: 7 P.M. each Thursday, Room 106 in Classroom Building Complex. Call for mailing list, 895-3547.

Las Vegas Natural History Museum: Fun, fun, fun. This museum, gift shop, and science store offers a hands-on room for kids, animated dinosaurs, marine life (featuring sharks), a diversity of birds, and an international wildlife room. This nonprofit organization is open from 9 A.M. to 4 P.M. daily and is located at 900 Las Vegas Boulevard North. Telephone: 384-3466.

Hoover Dam Tour: It's not free, but it's well worth the drive and the price. Take a thirty-five-minute guided tour of the inner workings of the dam. The tour runs daily from 8:30 A.M. to 5:45 P.M. all year. Price: adults, $5; seniors, $2.50; children 12 and under, free. And don't forget to visit the Snacketeria, a forty-seat snack bar near the dam.

Ethel M Chocolate Factory: In nearby Henderson, not far from Cranberry World, a free gourmet-chocolate factory tour awaits you. Watch the candy-making process from start to finish through windows while videos guide the tour. Each visitor receives a free Ethel M chocolate at the end of the tour—but only one! The two-and-a-half-acre cactus garden adjacent to the factory offers a variety of plant life. Hours: daily, 8:30 A.M. to 7 P.M. Drive east on Tropicana, right on Mountain Vista to Sunset Way, left into Green Valley Business Park, then left onto Cactus Garden Drive. Telephone: 458-8864.

13

Beyond the City Lights

A mule deer steps out from a stand of mahogany, glances your way, then continues browsing. You know you're not in Vegas anymore.

Although the city is likely never to lose its deserved image as a gambling town, inquisitive locals quickly learn that there is more to living in southern Nevada than green felt and neon.

Cynics might argue that Las Vegas is situated in the middle of nowhere, but enterprising residents long ago discovered that it is close to everywhere.

First, some geography. The sprawling mountain

range that forms the western wall of the valley is called the Spring Mountain Range, which stretches for fifty miles. Mount Charleston, at 11,918 feet, is the highest peak in the range and is snow-capped most of the year. On the opposite end of the valley stands Frenchman Mountain, also known as Sunrise Mountain. To the north, the Sheep Mountains. On the south, the Black and McCullough mountains complete the valley.

Mount Charleston

Now, about that mule deer. It is one of dozens of species that thrive in the Spring Mountain range. The wildlife and vegetation are a stark contrast to the desert floor just forty-five minutes away. The Toiyabe National Forest is noted not only for its pines, cedars, and bristlecones, but also for its thirty species of endemic plants. Dozens of hiking trails crisscross the mountains; the stout of heart will be challenged by a trip to Charleston Peak. For those who don't care to stray far from camp, there are many picnic areas and campsites for stays ranging from an afternoon to a month. Sites fill up early, so it is wise to make reservations. Call 873-8800.

In winter, the contrast with the desert is even greater, with plenty of snowfall in the higher elevations. On the Lee Canyon side is a full-service ski resort, Ski Lee, which has been pleasantly surprising downhillers and skiboarders since 1962. The small operation might pale in comparison to the larger resorts in California and Utah, but there is something to be said for fresh powder only forty minutes from Las Vegas.

If your idea of the call of the wild includes a fireplace and table service, then the Mount Charleston Hotel and Mount Charleston Lodge are more your speed. The hotel features a restaurant and lounge, and the lodge is known for its bar and weekend music.

The best-kept secret on Mount Charleston: Of the million-plus people who make the trip from Las Vegas to the mountain each year, perhaps one in 100 bypasses the lodge and hotel to experience the genuine wildlife to be found a few minutes off State Route 157. The hiking trails are seldom crowded.

Red Rock Canyon National Conservation Area

Head west on Charleston Boulevard approximately fifteen miles and you will reach the entrance to a site that rivals anything on the Strip. First-time visitors to Red Rock are awed by the towering sandstone escarpment that juts from the high desert in a mass of orange and red and tan. The 83,100-acre conservation area is highlighted by a thirteen-mile one-way loop that gives automobile sightseers a sample of the beauty and cyclists a genuine thrill. Burros, wild horses, prong-horned antelope, and desert bighorn sheep roam the area, and the sharp-eyed sometimes will catch a glimpse of migrating tarantulas and a wide variety of snakes, including a few of the venomous kind.

Although hiking trails are abundant, travelers often find themselves at Bonnie Springs Ranch for lunch or dinner, and Old Nevada for a taste of Hollywood's version of the Wild West. Bonnie Springs also offers a hotel, free petting zoo, a miniature train ride, and horseback riding.

Spring Mountain Ranch State Park, just up the road, is an ideal place to picnic and is the site of summer concerts and plays.

If you continue on, you will encounter Blue Diamond, a small community with a general store and its own occasional newspaper. Blue Diamond originally housed workers from a nearby gypsum mine, but has evolved into a bedroom community for Las Vegas. A bit of Blue Diamond trivia: the town originally was named Cottonwood after nearby Cottonwood Springs, a watering hole for travelers along the Old Spanish Trail.

Pahrump

On the way to Pahrump on State Route 160, at the summit of the Spring Mountains, is the tiny community of Mountain Springs. The Mountain Springs Bar is crowded on weekends and an ideal place to hear bluegrass music in summer.

Pahrump, sixty miles from Las Vegas, is fast becoming another commuter community. A generation ago, alfalfa and cotton farms were its trademarks. Today it has plenty of casinos, restaurants, grocery stores, and even a winery. It also lies in Nye County, where fireworks sales and brothels are legal.

The Pahrump Harvest Festival in September is a kick for country folks and city slickers alike with its rodeo, parade, carnival, and hoedown.

Jean, Goodsprings, Sandy Valley, Primm

Thirty miles west of Las Vegas on Interstate 15 lies Jean, with its two hotel-casinos and one of the state's medium-security prisons. Eight miles west on State Route 161 is Goodsprings, with its turn-of-the-century homesites and Pioneer Saloon. Goodsprings may not have looked like much in 1996, but it was southern Nevada's largest city as late as the 1920s. Six miles farther on 161, you will drop down into Sandy Valley. Like Pahrump, Sandy also is growing rapidly and becoming a popular place for southern Nevadans wishing to live outside the city lights. The town offers two bars, a cafe, a grocery store, and an entertaining parade and barbecue on the Fourth of July.

On the Nevada-California state line forty-five miles from Las Vegas is one of the area's grand entrepreneurial statements: a town built by one family, the Primms. Primm, Nevada, is named for gambler Ernie Primm, who settled on the border with a humble service station and a few slot machines. Although the place had been inhabited long before Primm arrived, he envisioned a desert oasis, complete with a hotel, casino, and restaurants. His son Gary carries on the family tradition with Whiskey Pete's, the Primadonna, and Buffalo Bill's, which features the breathtaking Desperado roller coaster.

Boulder City, Lake Mead, Hoover Dam

A dozen miles east of Las Vegas, just beyond the valley lies idyllic Boulder City. The "best town by a dam site" grew along with the construction of nearby Hoover Dam beginning in 1931, and until 1960 Boulder City remained under the control of the Bureau of Reclamation. Visitors quickly will notice a distinct lack of urban sprawl and slot machines there. In fact, gaming is not allowed within the city limits.

Its parks make ideal places to picnic, and the half-century-old Boulder Dam Hotel is one of the area's precious historic sites. Its restaurant serves superior Italian food, and the Arizona Street area is dotted with shops. The Boulder City/Hoover Dam Museum is a favorite with families.

Carved out of Black Canyon forty miles from Las Vegas, Hoover Dam remains one of the great wonders of Great Depression engineering and ingenuity. Hoover Dam's seventeen generators produce one-fourth the energy consumed by the Las Vegas valley. Most of the energy generated by the 726-foot-high, 660-foot-thick dam is used to power parts of Arizona and Southern California.

Hoover Dam cost $160 million to build in 1930s, and it was completed on time in a little more than four years. The estimated cost to build it today is $4 billion, but even that figure is deceiving. It does not take into account environmental laws and the usual government cost overruns. By way of example, the dam's new parking garage, visitors center, and elevators cost almost as much to construct as the original dam site.

The tour is well worth the long wait in line just for the opportunity to descend into the bowels of one of the nation's working wonders. The forty-four-story elevator ride is a thrill in itself, although claustrophobics might want to avoid it. Someone on your tour is sure to ask how many people were killed in the construction of the dam (ninety-six), and how many of those are entombed in the dam (none). The whole trip lasts 35 minutes and costs $5 for adults, $2.50 for seniors, and is free to children 12 and under.

Hoover Dam holds back Lake Mead, one of the largest man-made lakes in the world. Its 822-mile shoreline is dotted with nine marinas, which offer a variety of services. The lake is popular with boaters, campers, and anglers, who work the waters for striped and largemouth bass.

The massive Lake Mead National Recreation Area is composed of Lake Mead, Lake Mohave and the surrounding desert from Davis Dam to the south, Grand Canyon National Park to the east, and north to Overton. Nearly 90 percent of the recreation area is desert.

Although you'll find most of the sunbathers stretched out at Boulder Beach, the Alan Bible Visitors Center offers plenty of information on the lake and area's desert flora and fauna.

Recreation area fees are $5 per car per week or $15 for an annual pass.

A word of caution: The summer heat can be excruciating, running a full ten to fifteen degrees hotter than Las Vegas. Thunder storms are known to cause flash floods inside the recreation area, so plan ahead.

The lake has nine developed areas, including picnic sites, marinas, camping, and swimming spots. You will also find dinner cruises available on Lake Mead for reasonable rates.

Valley of Fire, Moapa Valley

Nevada's oldest state park remains one of its most breathtaking. Valley of Fire State Park was dedicated in 1935—practically prehistoric on the Las Vegas time line—and for generations visitors have marveled at its red sandstone rock formations and ancient Indian petroglyphs. The park offers campgrounds and a visitors' center.

Newcomers to the Valley of Fire will want to plan to be there during a full moon, when the night lighting sets the sandstone ablaze.

The Moapa Valley, which includes Moapa, Glendale, Overton, Logandale, Meadow Valley, the Moapa Indian Reservation, and Warm Springs, begins approximately fifty miles northeast of Las Vegas. The Clark County Fair in April highlights the year for Logandale.

Just south of Overton is the Lost City Museum, which houses a fascinating collection of Anasazi and Pueblo Indian artifacts. The Pueblos have inhabited the area for centuries, but newcomers   are welcome at the museum, which is open from 8:30 A.M. to 4:30 P.M. with $1 admission.

No matter which end of the valley you choose, southern Nevada offers much more than the Strip and downtown. Consider this merely a prologue to your own adventures beyond the city lights.

Stateline (Primm)

On the border of Nevada and California lies Primm with its three hotel-casinos—the Primadonna Resort and Casino, Whiskey Pete's Hotel-Casino, and Buffalo's Bill's Resort and Casino. Buffalo's Bill's is likely the destination of choice. This sixteen-story hotel and casino offers a 200-seat Victorian-style movie theater (with first-run movies); a 6,500-seat special events arena (for their popular concerts and rodeos); the Desperado roller coaster; and a 650-seat showroom. Also available are restaurants and a buffet. Drive forty miles south of Las Vegas on Interstate 15. Telephone: 382-1111.

Death Valley

If you have a trustworthy vehicle, Death Valley National Park is a fun daylong excursion. The length of the park is 140 miles, with many attractions along the way. One such place is Furnace Creek Visitors' Center, where you can find maps and brochures describing Death Valley; also nature exhibits and slide shows and restrooms are available here.

Badwater is the lowest point in the United States at 280 feet below sea level. The Harmony Borax Works is an interesting trail that leads to an abandoned borax mine. Death Valley Junction, population seven, is the location of the Amargosa Opera House, where Marta Becket performs a one-woman dance show about ninety-five times per year.

Scotty's Castle, formerly known as the Death Valley Ranch, is a twenty-five-room mansion admired for its fine craftsmanship. It was built near a stream, which provided its occupants with water and power. Tours are conducted every hour, daily.

For a good time at Death Valley Junction, visit the Crow Bar, an old-time bar with few patrons. Sit at the bar and talk to people from all around the world.

Also available up the road from Death Valley Junction is Tecopa Hot Springs, a popular spot for senior citizens. Visit the public bathing houses (separated by sex). No swimsuits allowed, so bring your sense of humor.

Laughlin

This boomtown is like a small Las Vegas. One hundred twenty miles south of town on State Route 163, Laughlin offers more than 8,500 hotel rooms at very inexpensive rates during the week (as low as $19). Las Vegans consider it a dressed-down alternative to the glitzier hotel-casinos in Las Vegas. It boasts only one movie theater, but many of the hotels offer first-rate concerts. Laughlin sits on the Colorado River; some hotels offer riverboat rides.

14

Quickie Marriages and Abiding Faith

Many visitors find it odd that religious worship takes place in Las Vegas, a place that gives off such secular vibes, but that's one of the city's many ironies.

Another long-perpetuated myth about Las Vegas is that it has more churches per capita than any other city in America. The remark has found its way into print in dozens of newspapers and many books, and it made for a great comeback when moralists were busy beating up Las Vegas and calling it Sin City and the Devil's Playground, but it's just not the case.

Las Vegas does, however, lead the planet in places to get married. The highest wedding chapels are located at the 1,149-foot Stratosphere Tower on Las Vegas Boulevard. The most famous chapel in the city is the Little Chapel of the West near the Hacienda, and perhaps the funkiest chapel in the city is the Graceland Wedding Chapel, which features an Elvis theme and offers a minister who vaguely resembles the Man from Memphis.

Another misconception is the idea that the Mormon faith makes up a large percentage of church-goers in the valley. That, too, is false. Although the Mormons might make a strong argument for their devotion to their church, their numbers make up just 6 percent of the Las Vegas population. What they lack in numbers, however, they more than make up for in places to worship. In fact, there are more Mormon churches, 164 in 1994, than any other religious faith in southern Nevada. In fact, there are more Mormon churches than there are Catholic, Methodist, Jewish, and Lutheran places of worship combined. The church also features by far the most recognizable edifice for miles in the form of the Mormon Temple at the base of Frenchman Mountain at the east end of the valley.

Here are the numbers:

Catholic	*28 percent*
Protestant	*27 percent*
No Affiliation	*22 percent*
Other	*13 percent*
Mormon	*6 percent*
Jewish	*5 percent*

Religious organizations are also numerous, such as the Salvation Army, Catholic Daughters of the

Americas, Jewish Federation of Las Vegas, St. Jude's Women's Auxiliary, etc. Also there are twenty-five stores that could be called religious bookstores.

Two radio stations offer religious broadcasting: KILA (90.5 FM) and KKVV (1060 AM).

New residents who settle on the outer edges of the valley may have difficulty finding a specific house of worship close to them. In this boomtown, Sunday morning commutes to church are common occurrences.

If you didn't have faith, you probably wouldn't have had the courage to move to a boomtown.

15

For Consumers

Las Vegas is a shopper's paradise, but it wasn't always that way. Only a few years ago, the city's population—despite the millions of tourists who visited each year—did not warrant serious attention from the upscale department stores that proliferate larger cities. There were plenty of Sears and JCPenney stores in the local malls and an assortment of specialty shops at the resorts offering furs and custom Italian leather goods, but the finer shops were hard to find.

All that changed as southern Nevada approached the million population mark. It also helped that, in some cases, managers of many major chains began to market toward tourists as well as locals. The result has been an explosion of shopping outlets that are good and getting better. They might even make you feel as if you've never left home.

The valley's leading malls:

The Boulevard Mall: This is Las Vegas's largest (and oldest) mall. Shops include the Nature Company, Sears, JCPenney, Dillards, Victoria's Secret, and Hot Dog on a Stick. This is a wonderful mall for strolling and people-watching, as well as shopping. 3768 South Maryland Parkway. Hours: Monday to Friday, 10 A.M. to 9 P.M.; Saturday, 10 A.M. to 7 P.M.; Sunday, 11 A.M. to 6 P.M.

Fashion Show Mall: Located on the Strip at Spring Mountain and Twain, the Fashion Show Mall has more than 100 specialty stores, including the Disney Store, Bally of Switzerland, Sharper Image, and Louis Vuitton. This is an upscale shopper's paradise—fun to stroll around, but unless you are wealthy, you will do more window-shopping than buying. Hours: Monday to Friday, 10 A.M. to 9 P.M.; Saturday, 10 A.M. to 7 P.M.; and Sunday, noon to 6 P.M. Telephone: 369-8382.

Forum Shops at Caesars: More than seventy shops and restaurants featuring Guess?, Gucci, the Museum Company, Spago, Planet Hollywood, and the Palm Restaurant. This is a must-see attraction, if only for the ceiling. This is also a super-upscale mall, so bring lots of money or just stroll around. Location: 3500 Las Vegas Boulevard South. Telephone: 893-4800.

Las Vegas Factory Stores of America Outlet Center: Located on the south end of Las Vegas Boulevard, the Las Vegas Factory Stores boast fifty factory-direct outlets, including Geoffrey Beene, B.U.M. Equipment, Lee, Wrangler, Jansport, Converse, and Adolfo II. You can find some good deals here if you really look. Take Las Vegas Boulevard five miles south of Tropicana. Hours: Monday to Saturday, 10 A.M. to 8 P.M.; Sunday, 10 A.M. to 6 P.M. Telephone: 897-9090.

Meadows Mall: This mall has easy access to I-15 (take the Valley View exit). Stores include Macy's, JCPenney, Sears, and more than 140 exciting shops and restaurants. This mall is a nice neighborhood mall and has shops whose prices are within reality. Hours: Monday to Friday, 10 A.M. to 9 P.M.; and weekends, 10 A.M. to 6 P.M. .

Galleria Mall: The city's newest mall, the Galleria is located in Green Valley, on Stephanie Street between Sunset Road and Warm Springs Road. Shops include Mervyn's California, Baby Gap, Dillards, JCPenney. An excellent food court. Take I-95 south to Sunset.

Belz Factory Outlet World Mall: Down the street from the other factory outlet. Includes Bass, Geoffrey Beene, Levi's, Oshkosh, Ruff Hewn, Corning-Revere, Nike. The latest expansion to this mall almost doubled its size. A very nice mall to look for good deals on top-name items.

Swap Meets

There is one outdoor swap meet, the Broadacres at the corner of Las Vegas Boulevard North and Lamb in North Las Vegas. This twenty-six-acre shopping area is open Friday, Saturday, and Sunday, with admission 50 cents on Friday and 75 cents on weekends. You will find both new and used merchandise, but arrive early for the best deals. Opens at 6:30 A.M.

There are two indoor swap meets, selling all new merchandise: the Fantastic Indoor Swap Meet, on the west side of town at 1717 South Decatur Boulevard, and the Boulder-Sahara Indoor Swap Meet, 3455 Boulder Highway on the east side of town.

Antiques and Crafts

Charleston Boulevard is the center of the antique universe in Las Vegas. Most shops are found there. Just drive down East Charleston, between Maryland Parkway and Eastern, and you will find dozens of antique stores.

A few stores stand out as especially fun or interesting places to shop.

The Red Rooster is a great place, but only go if you have at least two hours to spare. This 25,000-square-foot consignment store offers antiques, unique gifts, and handmade crafts of all kinds. Location: 1109 Western Avenue. Can be difficult to find for newcomers unacquainted with the winding back streets near Charleston Boulevard and Martin Luther King Drive. Go east on Charleston, right on

Martin Luther King, left on Wall Street, left on Western. Hours: Monday to Saturday, 10 A.M. to 6 P.M.; Sunday, noon to 5 P.M.

The Gypsy Caravan, at the corner of Maryland Parkway and Charleston, is open Monday to Saturday 10 A.M. to 6 P.M., Sunday noon to 5 P.M. This large store offers antiques of all kinds, including antique furniture.

Garage Sales

Garage sales are numerous in Las Vegas and a great way to spend an early Saturday or Sunday morning. You can find real bargains if you check the Friday night or Saturday morning ads (early!) and circle those sales you think will have things you want. Then plan a route and go to each of those sales. Garage sale ads in the *Review-Journal* are separated by territory, and Las Vegas is divided into four: southwest, northwest, southeast, northeast.

Epilogue

Outside Views: Hollywood and the Media

If you watch the movies, then you know the score. Vegas isn't a town, it's a virus. It's a deceit-stained dice pit lined with foul-mouthed mobsters, coked-up strippers, and booze-addled dreamers.

Every pass is snake eyes here in the land of the neon sun. The game is rigged. Sisyphus rolls these crooked dice time after time.

Even Dante would fear Vegas—at least the one portrayed on the big screen.

Las Vegas has long been a favorite setting for

Hollywood, but in the mid-1990s, the dark themes pouring forth from the city onto the screen were downright disturbing. From Martin Scorsese's mob epic *Casino*, Mike Figgis's darkly artistic Charter Hospital commercial *Leaving Las Vegas*, and Paul Verhoeven's unmentionable backhanded tribute to the city's silicone sisters *Showgirls*, you can understand what makes the squares at the Las Vegas Chamber of Commerce run for the Maalox. It's a wonder the phones at southern Nevada's Suicide Prevention Hotline don't ring off the hook.

The fact is, they sometimes do, but it's not the movies that concern Las Vegas residents. It's the reality of living in the fastest-growing community in America on the cusp of the twenty-first century that can take its toll on residents.

With few exceptions, the movies that pour forth from the city are awash in vice and blood, skinny girls and big guns. To Hollywood's directorial grifters, it's that kind of town. It's easy to see the city as the average tourist sees it: From the Strip to downtown, the joint is one lusty, seething big-budget movie set with the bright lights and dark magic built in.

But, unless you're playing, gambling is pretty boring. That's a big reason why, for all the dozens of movies that have been set in Las Vegas, so few of the good ones have anything to do with cards and dice. They're props; the characters are what make the city a case for study.

The characters were part of what used to make Las Vegas a great place to live. This place ought to have been Runyon's winter home. The guys and dolls not only hung out in the casinos, but they also shopped at the Safeway and lived in quiet neighborhoods and sent their kids to school here.

Most of that has changed. With more than 1 million people living in the metropolitan area—and the population expected to double in a decade—Las Vegas isn't just a surrealistic roadside rest stop anymore. With more than 30 million visitors converging on the city—and $5.7 billion in gaming revenue generated countywide—the city rivals Disney World as the nation's top tourist destination.

Problem is, Las Vegas has not yet emerged from intense therapy. It's made strides, but still suffers from an inferiority complex and all-world growing pains. Problem is, Las Vegas is not just like every other maturing metropolis. The casino lifestyle has something to do with it, but many of the problems are attributable to a single factor.

It's the growth. Las Vegas is America's last great boomtown, and the casinos comprise the Comstock Lode. The city perennially ranks at or near the top of the fastest-growing category. That's good news for developers, who have built thousands of houses and apartments to accommodate the legions of monied retirees and short-pockets service workers who have invaded in Joad family fashion in search of good jobs and warm winters.

That's the Las Vegas story. It's not as lascivious as *Showgirls* or as bloody as *Casino*, but growth—with all its blessings and curses—is the greater reality around these parts.

Nevada led the nation last year in personal-income growth and ranks ninth in per-capita income. In 1995, nearly 19,500 homes were built in the valley to accommodate the four thousand people who move here each month. That's the good news.

The state leads the nation in other categories as well. Crime, for instance. Nevada topped the country with a 13 percent increase in 1994, according to the FBI's annual report.

But all this success may be toughest on the children: highest teen suicide rate, second highest teen pregnancy rate. Nevada is last in the nation in aid to preschool children and has the fourth-highest teen-death rate and the highest juvenile incarceration rate in America. It also has the highest high school dropout rate in America.

The state also leads the nation in alcohol consumption and smoking, and the Las Vegas valley battles a lack of public parks and an air quality problem that ranks it among the country's worst cities.

The dilemma in education might be the greatest problem facing southern Nevada's future. The state's libertarian, laissez-faire business philosophy simply does not fit the vast needs of the population. The children of the boom are suffering, and it's something all newcomers to southern Nevada must consider. Clark County School District Superintendent Brian Cram was not exaggerating when he told community leaders that education is about opening doors and not about closing cell doors behind troubled teen-agers.

There's an element of truth to the Hollywood

image of Las Vegas as the mob's final frat house, Figgis's booze hell, and even Verhoeven's floozy fest. Its noire elements are seductive, and not only to tourists and movie producers. People really do get lost here.

It's also a place for second chances, the kind working people are willing to live and die and travel 3,000 miles to find. No one can blame Hollywood for missing the real Las Vegas story, but the growing pains of the nation's last great boomtown are no less compelling than any dark image drawn by Scorsese.

When you move to Las Vegas, you learn to accept the dark with the light.

Appendices

Just the Facts

Twenty Las Vegans you should know

Mayor Jan Jones The city's first woman mayor, Jones is a former automobile dealership executive who ran an unsuccessful race for governor.

Bob Stupak The former Vegas World Casino owner defines the word flamboyant. He dreamed up the idea for the 1,149-foot Stratosphere Tower, paid a man to jump off the top of his twenty-two-story hotel, once won a $1-million bet on the Super Bowl, survived more than one state Gaming Control Board inquiry into his business practices.

Steve Wynn With wildly successful resorts, a formidable political machine, and a willingness to force his will on elected officials, he is the current king of Las Vegas. Wynn's feuds with Atlantic City gaming figure Donald Trump as well as his increased interest in national issues and presidential politics has dramatically increased his public profile. He is the subject of the 1995 investigative biography, *Running Scared: The Life and Treacherous Times of Las Vegas Casino King Steve Wynn* written by John L. Smith and published by Barricade Books.

Harry Reid Born in Searchlight, Harry Reid is a southern Nevada success story. Overcoming a poor upbringing, Reid traveled 160 miles a day to and from high school, and now the Democrat is Nevada's senior senator.

Richard Bryan The U.S. senator is a fierce opponent of the federal government's attempt to put a nuclear waste repository at Yucca Mountain in central Nevada. Bryan has distinguished himself as a staunch advocate of his constituents. The Democrat was raised locally and worked in the Clark County Public Defender and District Attorney's offices.

Andre Agassi The champion professional tennis player not only is a longtime Las Vegan, but also makes a substantial contribution to the community through the Andre Agassi Foundation.

Greg Maddux The Valley High graduate is the

Cy Young Award–winning pitcher for the Atlanta
Braves and one of many Las Vegans to make a mark
in professional sports.

John Ensign The stepson of Circus Circus executive Mike Ensign, John burst onto the political
scene in 1994 when he upset incumbent James
Bilbray to win one of Nevada's two seats in the House
of Representatives.

Dr. Carol Harter UNLV's president took over for
the embattled Robert Maxson, whose tenure was
highlighted by unprecedented growth at the state
university but also was marred by a nasty fight with
legendary Runnin' Rebels basketball Coach Jerry
Tarkanian.

Bill Hanlon The longtime math instructor not
only teaches arithmetic at all levels, he also writes an
education column, conducts televised lessons on the
local public station, and is an outspoken member of
the State Board of Education.

Dr. Brian Cram The superintendent of the Clark
County School District is a former high school
teacher and principal and now has the difficult task
of guiding K-12 education in a boomtown.

Kirk Kerkorian The quiet billionaire, who is
responsible for building the largest hotel in the
world three times during his thirty-year Las Vegas
tenure, often is sighted at local restaurants dining in
near-anonymity.

Jerry Keller Clark County's sheriff is a Western High graduate who ascended the ranks of the Metropolitan Police Department and defeated venerable ex-sheriff Ralph Lamb for the job.

Bob Broadbent As the executive director of McCarran International Airport, Broadbent has shepherded the growth of the airport, one of the busiest and most efficient in America.

Bill Branon He is a popular local writer whose novels include Let Us Prey and Devil's Hole.

Sherman Frederick As the publisher of the *Las Vegas Review-Journal*, Nevada's largest newspaper, Frederick carries substantial political clout.

Kenny Guinn The former superintendent of schools is a retired corporate executive whose name often is mentioned on the short list of candidates for governor.

Dina Titus The UNLV political science professor and author leads Democrats in the state senate.

Patricia Mulroy As the executive director of the Las Vegas Water Authority and head of the Las Vegas Valley Water District, Mulroy is one of the most powerful figures in the state.

Brian Greenspun The eldest son of late *Las Vegas Sun* publisher Hank Greenspun, Brian is an attorney who heads his family's publishing, cable television, and development dynasty. As a former classmate of Bill Clinton, Greenspun played an important role in communicating the interests of Nevadans and the casino industry to the White House.

Jackie Gaughan Patriarch of the Gaughan gambling family, whose local casinos include Barbary Coast and son Michael Gaughan's Gold Coast, Jackie Gaughan arrived in Las Vegas in 1946 and now owns six downtown casinos.

Twenty-five Dates in Las Vegas History

11000 B.C.	Near the site of Las Vegas, human beings live and hunt.
1843 A.D.	John C. Fremont begins mapping territory that would become Nevada
1855	Mormon missionaries open a mission in Las Vegas
1857	Mormon missionaries close their mission in Las Vegas
1864	Nevada admitted to Union as the thirty-sixth state
1905	Las Vegas becomes a townsite
1911	Las Vegas officially becomes a city
1931	Governor signs six-week divorce law
1931	Gambling legalized in Nevada
1941	The first resort on the Las Vegas Strip—the El Rancho—opens; the El Cortez opens downtown

1946	Ben Siegel's Flamingo opens
1947	Ben Siegel murdered in Beverly Hills
1950	The Desert Inn opens
1951	First atomic weapon tested at Nevada Test Site; Benny Binion opens the Horseshoe Club
1952	The Sands and Sahara open
1954	The Showboat opens
1955	The Dunes and Riviera open
1957	Nevada Southern University (now University of Nevada, Las Vegas) erects its first permanent building
1958	Las Vegas Convention Center opens
1963	McCarran Airport opens
1966	Caesars Palace opens
1968	Circus Circus opens
1969	International Hotel (now the Las Vegas Hilton) opens
1973	MGM Grand (now Bally's) opens
1990	Landmark Hotel demolished to create additional parking for Las Vegas Convention Center

Ten Las Vegans from the Past:

William Clark The Montana senator's railroad went through southern Nevada in the early twentieth century and led to the development of Las Vegas as a city.

Benjamin "Bugsy" Siegel The best-known, and perhaps most overrated, influence on Las Vegas, Siegel was murdered at the Beverly Hills home of galpal Virginia Hill in June 1947. Siegel is credited, wrongly, with the idea for the Flamingo Hotel. No one called him Bugsy while he was alive without regretting it.

Moe Dalitz One of the founding fathers of the real Las Vegas, Dalitz was a Cleveland bootlegger with strong ties to Jimmy Hoffa's Teamsters Central States Pension Fund, who nevertheless migrated to Las Vegas and built not only casinos but hospitals and shopping malls as well. One of the great influences in Las Vegas history.

Gus Greenbaum The man who took over for Benny Siegel met an equally violent demise in 1955, when killers cut his throat and that of his wife.

Benny Binion The patriarch of the Binion's Horseshoe Club casino family, Benny was a Dallas rackets boss who admitted killing several men before coming to Las Vegas, where cards and dice were legal. A statue of Binion on horseback graces downtown.

Jay Sarno The big-idea man behind Caesars Palace and Circus Circus, Sarno was one of the grandest, and least known, entrepreneurs in the history of the city.

Grant Sawyer Perhaps Nevada's most important governor, Sawyer's political expertise guided the gaming industry away from federal scrutiny and toward state regulation.

Tony Cornero This gambling boss operated casino ships off California and came to Las Vegas with a dream of building what became known as the Stardust. Cornero ran out of money and friends, and ended up dying of a heart attack at a Desert Inn crap table.

Howard Hughes The eccentric billionaire occupied the ninth floor of the Desert Inn Hotel and bought seven casinos, but today his greatest impact is felt in the planned community developments at Summerlin in the northwest section of the valley.

Rex Bell, Sr. The former Nevada lieutenant governor was married to silent-movie star Clara Bow. The Bell family once had a ranch near Nipton, California, close to the Nevada stateline called the Walking Box.

Twenty-five Nevada Facts

- Richest person: Forrest E. Mars, Sr.; more than $3 billion.
- Native born Nevadans number only 21.8 percent.
- Nevada has 3,380 blackjack tables.
- Largest city in Nevada: Las Vegas; next largest, Reno.
- Population growth rate from 1980 to 1990: 50.38 percent.
- Nevada's area is 110,540 square miles.
- Nevada ranks seventh in state size.

- Halloween is a state holiday in Nevada because it happens to fall on its date of admission to the Union: 31 October, 1864.
- Median age: 34.2.
- Population: 1,592,000.
- Nevada was once part of the Republic of Mexico. It was ceded to the United States in 1848 as part of the Treaty of Guadalupe Hidalgo.
- Amount of Nevada land federally-owned: 83 percent.
- Highest point: Boundary Peak in Esmeralda County—13,143 feet.
- State bird: mountain bluebird.
- State flower: shrub sagebrush.
- State tree: single-leaf pinion pine; also bristlecone pine.
- State motto: "All for our country."
- State nicknames: Silver State; Sagebrush State; Battle Born State (it became a state during the Civil War).
- State animal: bighorn sheep.
- State song: "Home Means Nevada" by Bertha Raffetto.
- State fish: Lahonton cutthroat trout.
- State reptile: desert tortoise.
- State rock: sandstone.
- State grass: Indian rice grass.
- State metal: silver.

INDEX